DAD, I'M COUNTING

ON

YOU!

How To Be A Hero In Your Baby's First 12 Months

By

Brad Wells

ISBN: 979-8-9920220-3-2

Printed in

First Edition, 2025

TABLE OF CONTENTS

INTRODUCTION

There I was at 2:13 in the morning, a tiny baby staring up at me with big, blinking eyes. That's when I noticed my shirt was covered in spit-up. The baby had been hiccupping for two hours, and I was starting to wonder if that was normal. For the hundredth time that night, I hoped a secret manual was hidden somewhere in the house. Spoiler alert: there wasn't.

Once I was completely overwhelmed and exhausted, I realized that this is how the first 24 hours must be for most new dads. Prenatal classes and YouTube videos are great, but they don't prepare you for when the baby is actually in your living room. I know you want to be the hero your kid deserves and get everything right.

Those of you reading this are either in the middle of it, about to be in it, or still coming out of it. You might not feel like it yet, but you're a new dad. Maybe you feel like a guy in sweats with a baby tucked under one arm, unsure if you even brushed your teeth today. You're not alone, and you're not supposed to know everything. That's why I wrote this book.

This book is different. It won't tell you to just ask your partner or let mom handle it. This book is hands-on and practical. It will make you laugh when you need to. It's a survival guide for dads who want to be involved. It's for guys who want to jump in and get their hands dirty so they can be a dad their kid can look up to. Remember, it might take changing a diaper with one eye open at four in the morning.

I care because I've talked to hundreds of dads and read the research. I learned the difference between what works and what doesn't. I dedicated myself to helping first-time fathers. I have a passion for helping first-time fathers. I know it's easy to feel lost, left out. I want you to feel confident and included. I want you to take charge, no matter what life and your baby might throw at you.

How worried are you? Let's be honest, you're probably terrified of messing up. Are you worried that you can't calm down a screaming baby? Are you worried you'll say the wrong thing to your partner? So what if you're the only dad at daycare who can't fold a stroller? At this point, you're probably drowning in advice from all over. Trust me, you'll hear from family, friends, and even strangers in the diaper aisle. You might feel pressure to be the perfect dad, even if you have no idea what that really means.

Most parenting books aren't much help for dads. They're usually written with moms in mind. Some of the advice is so generic it could apply to raising a turtle. Others still lean on outdated stereotypes that don't reflect today's families. What you need is something different, something that speaks to you as a dad living in the modern world. That's what this book is all about.

Time to learn about "Dad Mode". I'm not making this up. It's a way of thinking that allows you to show up, learn fast, and not wait for permission. Dad Mode means you're in action, not on the sidelines. You take the shot knowing that you will miss sometimes.

This book is full of help you can use right now. You'll find checklists for every stage and dad hacks that actually work. You'll even get stories from dads who've been there. How would you like a month-by-month guide that walks you through the whole first year? Get real information on crying, sleep, bonding with your baby, and supporting your partner. Learn why swaddling isn't always the answer. This is a quick reference tool when you really need it.

Every kind of dad should see himself in these pages. Whether you're a single dad, part of a two-dad family, an adoptive dad, or a first-time dad at 45, this is for you. This book represents all dads and all kinds of families. You'll get real and practical advice even if your family is not like the ones you see on TV.

You might not believe it, especially if you've already tried other books full of fluff. But this one will give you the answers you need, fast. No filters, no sugarcoating. We'll get you through the night, the week, and your wild first year.

You can expect to have confidence from day one. You'll learn step-by-step skills in case you've never held a baby before. Learn to support your partner and take care of your own mental health. On top of that, you'll learn to balance work, money, and family. I'm giving you a roadmap for surviving while you enjoy these twelve beautiful and sometimes frustrating months.

I want you to get involved, not just read the pages. You can watch your baby grow by using the milestone tracker. Remember to fill out the 'Dad Win' pages and celebrate every victory. Start telling your stories. Join a community of new dads. I'm sure they're figuring it out one day, one diaper, and one bottle at a time.

I promise you're not alone and you're more capable than you think. Let this book be your go-to guide for the first year. This is Dad Mode. Your hero's journey starts now.

CHAPTER 1

Launching Dad Mode: Your First 24 Hours and Survival Week

Picture this: you walk in, baby carrier in one hand, hospital bag in the other, and your house suddenly feels foreign. The car seat still smells new. Your partner looks relieved but exhausted. You can't help thinking, "Who let me leave with a human?" It feels like someone in scrubs should chase you down and quiz you, but nobody does. Now, it's just you, your partner, and a tiny person making brand-new noises.

This is when Dad Mode begins. Not because you're ready, but because now you're the one to find answers. Most dads expect to feel prepared; few actually are. The first 24 hours are a blur of questions: how to hold, feed, and change your baby (a lot, by the way). You'll fuel yourself on adrenaline and pocket snacks.

The first week is overwhelming: cluster feeding (baby seems to eat non-stop), epic diaper blowouts, and emotions running high for both you and your partner. At 3 a.m., when you're exhausted and unsure, remember: nobody has it all together at first. This chapter is here to turn panic into purpose and give you a nitty-gritty playbook for those first days in Dad Mode.

Dad Mode On: Your 24-Hour Quick Start Plan

Here's what those first 24 hours at home look like. Keep things simple. Settle your baby into a safe sleep spot such as a crib, bassinet, or cot (hopefully already set up). Make sure diapers, wipes, onesies, and burp cloths are within reach. A snack and coffee station for parents is a lifesaver, especially for those bleary-eyed middle-of-the-night feedings.

Early on, you'll tackle your first diaper change. Lay out everything you need, such as wipes, fresh diaper, cream, and keep a hand on the baby to prevent escaping. Newborns are squirmy, and that first black-tar poop (meconium) is strange but normal. Don't stress about speed; you'll get quicker with practice (Diaper Changing Tips).

Then comes feeding. Babies eat often and unpredictably at first. Cluster feeding is when they eat almost hourly for hours; it's normal but exhausting. Be supportive if your partner is breastfeeding by offering snacks, water, and encouragement. If you're bottle feeding, having clean bottles ready saves time.

Take advantage of nap time, not just for the baby but for you and your partner too. Don't feel bad if you both zonk out on the couch while the baby sleeps in their safe space. It's survival, not slacking.

Fatigue reaches its peak by evening. The night shift is Dad Mode's proving ground: dim lights, quiet voices, and minimal stimulation help baby sort out day from night. Calm, quiet routines at night reassure your baby and your partner.

Emotions can surge after sunset. "Witching hour" fussiness is real, and so are the mood swings from both parents and the baby. Tears and frustration are normal.

Dad Mode isn't about always being confident; it's about pressing on even when you're uncertain. Your main job: tune

3

in to your baby and partner, stay calm, and adapt when things go sideways.

Prepare a "baby zone" before you come home. Group essentials like diapers, wipes, onesies, and burp cloths together. Post emergency contacts where everyone will see them (fridge or charging station). Keep snacks and drinks within easy reach; nobody parents well when they're hangry.

Here's a dad hack: stash granola bars and water bottles in any area you might end up feeding or calming your baby during overnight shifts. Another: keep a notebook or whiteboard handy to jot down questions or reminders when you're half-awake.

Thoughts like "Is the baby breathing?" or "Was that noise normal?" are completely common and temporary. Every new dad has them.

If you find yourself joining "Team No Sleep," remember you're in good company. There are dads everywhere wandering around bleary-eyed, sipping cold coffee, and puzzling over baby gear.

Perfection isn't expected or required. Dad Mode is about showing up, again and again, even when you're exhausted, confused, or doubting yourself. That's what matters for your partner, for your baby, and for you.

The Essential "Don't Panic" Dad Checklist

Standing in your hallway after that hospital escape, you might freeze, unsure where to start. Newborns don't wait for you to get your bearings; they need food, clean butts, and a safe place to snooze. Everything else can wait. To keep the chaos from swallowing you, here's a straight-shooting checklist that gets you through the first night and week without losing your mind. Tape it to the fridge, screenshot it for your phone, or scrawl it on the back of a takeout menu. This is not about perfection, just keeping the basics rolling.

Dad Checklist: First Night and Week

- **Feeding Log:**
  - Mark each feeding (time, left/right if breastfeeding, or ounces if bottle).
  - Note spit-up, burps, and any "refusals."

- o Track diapers after feeds; pee and poop both count.
- **Diaper Station Setup:**
  - o Stash at least 10-12 diapers within arm's reach.
  - o Wipes (open package before baby arrives, trust me).
  - o Diaper cream/tube handy for red butts.
  - o Two backup onesies because accidents happen in streaks.
  - o Spare plastic bags or a diaper pail for the stink bombs.
- **Partner Wellness Check:**
  - o Ask directly: "How are you feeling?" and mean it.
  - o Offer snacks, water, or a break.
  - o Keep any necessary meds, pads, or supports close for easy access.
  - o Remind them they're not alone in this.
- **Sleep Setup:**
  - o Baby's crib or bassinet should be clear of toys, pillows, and blankets, with just a fitted sheet.
  - o Nightlight for low-key check-ins.

- Your own pillow/blanket nearby for crash-landings between shifts.

Here's the real secret: don't waste your nerves on things that simply don't matter this week. That pile of laundry? Ignore it unless you've run out of burp cloths. Forget about deep cleaning the kitchen or alphabetizing the freezer. Elaborate baby schedules are pointless in week one; your newborn is running the show, and the script changes every hour. Grocery trips can wait unless you're out of diapers, wipes, or coffee.

New dads get tripped up by panic points that seem like emergencies but usually aren't. Non-stop crying will make your heart race, but babies cry for reasons as simple as being tired, hungry, overstimulated, or needing a fresh diaper. If the checklist isn't solving it, try:

- Check diaper (sometimes it's just wet).
- Offer food even if they just ate. Cluster feeding is real.
- Burp your baby with gentle pats on the back while supporting their head.
- Walk around holding your baby upright (gravity helps with gas).

- Dim the lights and lower the noise; sometimes babies just want calm.

If spit-up happens, and it will, don't stress unless it's projectile or green or yellow every time. Most newborns spit up after feeds because their digestive systems are still learning the ropes. Wipe baby down, swap outfits if needed, and keep burp cloths close.

If your baby won't latch while breastfeeding, try skin-to-skin contact for a few minutes, gently tickle their cheek to encourage rooting, and stay calm because babies pick up on stress fast. If you're bottle feeding and they refuse, check the temperature or try a different nipple size.

Blowout Protocol: When you open a diaper and find a situation that looks like a crime scene, don't panic. Lay everything out before you begin. Use wipes liberally; there's no prize for thriftiness in this battle. Roll up the old diaper underneath the baby as you work, so you have a clean landing zone. If things go sideways, literally, just breathe and remember that every dad has been christened by a blowout at least once.

Knowing what not to worry about will save your sanity. Don't obsess over whether your baby is sleeping "enough." Newborns sleep in strange patterns; charts and averages don't matter yet. Don't compare your baby (or yourself) to anyone else on social media because filters hide the messier truth. Most importantly, don't beat yourself up if things feel clumsy or awkward; all new dads start out that way.

Some newborn quirks are totally normal: hiccups that last forever, sneezing fits, jerky arm movements, noisy breathing (as long as there's no blue coloring or struggling for air). Red flags that do need quick action include fever over 100.4°F (38°C), refusal to eat for more than two feeds in a row, blue lips or skin, trouble breathing (not just noisy), or limpness that doesn't improve when awake. Call your pediatrician right away if you spot any of these.

Dad Wins Reflection Box

Jot down the small stuff that went right each day, even if it's as simple as "got baby to sleep without drama" or "kept my cool during a meltdown." These tiny wins are proof: you're getting better at this every hour. They'll keep you going when fatigue wants to take over and doubt creeps in.

Tag-Teaming: How to Rock the First Night with Your Partner

That first night at home, you and your partner are running on excitement, nerves, and maybe a little caffeine. Suddenly, reality hits: this tiny human needs care around the clock, and there's no shift change coming. Here's where true tag-teaming begins. Forget the idea that one parent is "better" or should do more; this is a partnership, not a contest.

Divide and conquer is your new mantra. You hand off the baby like a football after a feed, or swap places at the changing table, so nobody gets stuck with the same job all night. If you're prepping bottles, one of you can wash and fill while the other does a quick diaper check or rocks the baby. When the baby cries for the third time in an hour, calling out, "Your turn for baby jail duty!" can break the tension and get you both laughing instead of arguing.

Setting up a routine from the start, maybe alternating feeds or taking turns on diaper duty, keeps resentment at bay and gives each of you brief but necessary breaks.

Communication becomes survival gear, not just a nice idea. When one of you is fading fast or patience is thin, clear signals are vital. A simple "I need five minutes" or "Can you take over?" is often all it takes to prevent a meltdown, yours or the baby's. Sometimes, you just need a break to step outside or splash cold water on your face. Having code words or gestures helps too. Maybe it's a thumbs up for "I'm good" or a hand on the shoulder for "I'm about to lose it." Don't be afraid to say what you need; mind-reading doesn't work at 3 a.m.

Scripts help when words are hard to find in the fog of sleep deprivation. Try these: "What do you need right now?" opens the door for honesty without blame. "Want me to take over for a bit?" shows empathy and teamwork. Or keep it light with, "You do diapers, I'll handle negotiations with our tiny dictator." Humor diffuses tension better than any deep breath app. Even just saying, "We're doing our best" out loud can settle nerves and remind you both that nobody gets graded on style points tonight.

Resentment grows when one person feels they're carrying too much. Maybe you catch yourself thinking, "Why am I always doing this?" It happens to everyone, even with the best intentions. The myth that moms have some secret code for babies leads to dads feeling sidelined or clueless. This isn't true; skills come from practice, not chromosomes.

I've heard from dads who felt like background extras in their own homes until they started taking nighttime shifts or bottle feeds. One dad I know told me he never felt like a real parent until he took over every other night so his partner could sleep; by week two, he knew his baby's different cries and started volunteering for the night shift. Another dad shared that he and his husband rotated roles every feeding, one did the bottle, the other changed diapers, so nobody felt stuck or left out.

Quick nightly check-ins work wonders. After the baby finally nods off (even if it's only for 23 minutes), sit together for five minutes and ask: "What worked tonight? What should we tweak tomorrow?" These huddles aren't about blame; they're your chance to adjust game plans as a team. Maybe you realize that swapping jobs every two hours helps both of you stay sane, or that prepping bottles before bed means less stumbling around in the dark at midnight. Celebrate any win, no matter how small, before crashing for some rest. A high-five, fist bump, or even just a whispered "We survived!" cements your teamwork.

Starting a "parent win" ritual can become something you look forward to each day. Maybe you share one thing that went well, like "I kept my cool during the meltdown," "You got her to burp in record time," "We didn't argue about whose turn it was." Little victories matter more than perfect routines.

Tag-teaming isn't always smooth; sometimes miscommunication happens, tempers flare, or one person feels invisible. Don't let those moments define your partnership. Reset as needed, step back in, apologize quickly if needed, and move forward knowing every team has rough nights. The goal isn't perfect harmony; it's having each other's backs when things get loud and messy.

If you ever feel frustration rising, remember: this is not about keeping score. It's about surviving together and sharing both the chaos and the quiet moments. Nobody keeps track of who did more; what matters is nobody feels alone doing it all. The first night sets the tone for many more ahead;

working together now builds habits that will help you both down the road.

Baby's First Diaper: A No-Fear, No-Mess Guide

Changing your baby's diaper for the first time feels like being handed a bomb you're supposed to disarm while blindfolded. Your palms sweat, your mind races, and you wonder why nobody mentioned the weird stickiness of that first poop. The trick is to slow down and break the process into steps.

First, set up your changing station before you even open the diaper. Line up wipes, a clean diaper, a thin layer of diaper cream, and an extra onesie because leaks happen when you least expect them. Place your baby on a flat, stable surface (changing table, bed with a towel, or even the floor if you're desperate), and always keep one hand steady on your baby. Babies are wriggly, and they have a knack for rolling at the worst moments.

Open the dirty diaper slowly, pausing for any surprise sprays; little boys are notorious for launching a stream at inopportune times. Wipe gently from front to back for girls to prevent infection. Lift your baby's legs by the ankles with your free hand and slide the new diaper underneath before removing the old one, so you're ready if there's a last-minute eruption. Use wipes liberally, don't skimp, and immediately roll up the soiled diaper and wipes into a tight ball, sealing it before tossing it out.

Blowouts are their own beast. You'll know one when you see it: poop up the back, down the legs, maybe even in the hair. Stay calm. Strip baby down, wipe from top to bottom, and use as many wipes as necessary. If things get truly out of hand, run a warm washcloth or even give a quick bath. It's not about staying clean; it's about keeping your cool when chaos hits. Laugh if you can; one day this will be a story you tell at their wedding.

Odd colors like green or orange can pop up depending on what your partner eats while breastfeeding or from harmless bile changes. What matters more than color is how your baby seems—happy, eating well, no fever? You're good. Only worry if you see red (blood), chalky white (possible liver issue), or black after the first few days. In that case, call your pediatrician.

Speed and organization make diapers less stressful. A "dad hack" I swear by: set up multiple diaper caddies around the house; in the living room, bedroom, and car trunk with all the basics so you're never sprinting upstairs mid-meltdown. Keep plastic bags for dirty diapers handy in each spot. Practice pulling wipes out with one hand (trust me, you'll need that skill at 3 a.m.), and pre-open wipe packs so you're not fumbling with sticky tabs mid-change.

Worrying about hurting your baby or messing up is common; every dad I know has had those nerves at first. Babies are tougher than they look, but go gentle. Support their head and neck with your non-dominant hand when lifting legs; avoid yanking or twisting limbs. If you're nervous about cleaning sensitive spots or applying cream, go slow and talk to your baby as you work, even if they don't understand yet, your voice will calm both of you.

You will mess up sometimes. Maybe you stick the tabs wrong and have to start over while your baby pees on the clean diaper. Maybe you get poop on your own shirt (or worse). Everybody fumbles their first changes. One night I tried to wrestle a onesie over my daughter's head mid-blowout and somehow managed to get poop on my ear. Instead of panicking or feeling defeated, I just laughed. What else can you do? These mistakes don't make you a bad dad; they make you human.

The more you change diapers, the faster and more confident you'll become. Every time you succeed, no matter how clumsy it feels, you're building skills that matter. Tell yourself after each change: "I did it." You'll get quicker, cleaner, and less rattled each time until it's just another part of the day, like making coffee or tying your shoes.

Safely Handling and Soothing Your Newborn (Without Swaddling)

At first, handling your baby can make your arms feel too big and your hands unsure, but confidence develops quickly. Always move slowly, keeping one hand under your baby's head and neck, and the other supporting their bottom. Hold your baby close to your chest for comfort and stability. When picking up or putting down your baby, whether from a crib or changing table, slide a forearm behind their neck and upper back, scoop under their bottom with your other hand, and bring them close for warmth and calm.

The football hold is popular, especially for dads: place your baby along your forearm, body against your side, head in your palm facing out, legs behind. This provides great feeding support and lets you keep a hand free for multitasking. For soothing, the cross-body hold often works well—baby belly-down across both arms, head nuzzled in your elbow, feet over the opposite arm. When burping, drape the baby on your chest with their chin on your shoulder, or sit them upright on your lap; support the chest and head with one hand and gently tap their back with the other.

Swaddling was once a rite of passage, but now carries risks if not done just right. Babies who roll or are swaddled too loosely may get tangled, which isn't safe for sleep. The American Academy of Pediatrics now advises stopping swaddling once your baby shows signs of rolling. Alternatives like wearable sleep sacks with arm holes keep babies cozy but unrestricted. For calming before sleep, use other techniques: shushing near their ear (mimicking womb sounds), gentle rocking, and white noise machines or apps to mask distractions. Many newborns find comfort in a clean pacifier, though never force it.

Learning your newborn's cries is like cracking a secret code. With time, patterns become clear. A hungry cry builds up gradually, including "neh" sounds and rooting or sucking cues. Tired cries are rhythmic and whiny; look for red eyelids or yawns. Gas pain comes with sharp, short cries, knees pulled up, and a tense face. Overstimulation leads to high-pitched cries, flailing arms, and avoiding light or noise. Fast responses help: offer food for hunger cues, swaddle-free snuggle or rocking for tiredness, gentle tummy massages or bicycle legs for gas.

Swaddle fails are common; babies wriggle free, blankets slip, and anxieties rise. One of my first attempts ended with my daughter escaping both arms and feet in seconds. After that, I switched to a sleep sack and focused on her needs: my hand on her chest, soft humming, dim lights. Sleep sacks became the default; they kept her both warm and safe.

Most new dads have a story about botched swaddles, blankets on faces, and late-night panics. The breakthrough happens when you watch your baby's cues instead of sticking to strict routines. Sometimes soothing is just holding her upright, walking in a dim room, and whispering. Other times, it's a combination: pacifier, white noise, gentle sway, whatever works in the moment.

Every baby is different. Some like side-to-side rocking, others want to bounce gently on a yoga ball, regardless of your singing abilities. Try various holds and moves until you see what calms your baby. If it takes three techniques in five minutes to settle things down, that's normal. Parenting is about adapting, building confidence, and remembering that genuine connection matters more than perfect technique.

Quick Cry Decoder (Reference)

- **Hungry**: Rhythmic "neh" cries and rooting, offer food.
- **Tired**: Whimpers, eye rubbing, yawns, try rocking or gentle soothing.
- **Gassy**: Short, bursty cries with knees up, try burping or tummy massage.
- **Overstimulated**: High-pitched cries, turning away, move to a dark, quiet room, try soft shushing.

Trust yourself; you'll read these signals faster each day, and your handling will feel more natural. Your baby will feel your confidence grow. When nothing works, simply hold your baby close and breathe together until calm returns.

Real-World Dad Scenarios: Troubleshooting the First 48 Hours

Picture yourself slumped on the edge of the bed at 2 a.m., baby wailing so loud it rattles the window. You've tried rocking, feeding, checked the diaper, and even resorted to whispering a sports play-by-play just to fill the silence between cries. Nothing works. This is that "choose your own adventure" moment: do you freeze, tag in your partner, or run through a mental checklist? Most dads hit this wall early; what matters is how you move through it.

First, breathe (inhale for four, exhale for six). Scan for obvious issues: diaper (wet or dry?), hunger (last meal time?), gas (knees up, little tummy rub). If none of those click, try changing the scenery. Walk the hallway with the lights low, or head to the bathroom where the sound of running water hums in the background. Some babies just need a shift.

If that doesn't soothe, skin-to-skin contact often does wonders. If your baby's still inconsolable for more than two hours or shows signs of illness (fever, limpness, bluish color), call your pediatrician. Trust your gut, not just Google.

Decision trees can keep your mind steady when panic wants to take over. For endless crying:

- Start with comfort checks (diaper, feeding, burp).
- Next, try movement (rock, sway, walk).
- Then offer a pacifier or a gentle shushing sound.
- If nothing changes and your baby seems distressed (not just fussy), check for fever or odd breathing.
- Still worried? Make the call; no shame in asking for help.

Now, every dad has a confession. One night, I spent fifteen minutes hunting for a pacifier only to find it stuck to my sock. Another time, in a foggy haze, I put my baby's onesie on backward and only noticed when her feet poked out the neck hole. One dad I know panicked when his daughter sneezed fifteen times in a row, convinced she had some rare disease, when all she needed was a little nose suction and a cuddle. These mistakes aren't failures; they're proof you care enough to worry. Laugh at them when you can. Parenthood's hard enough without adding guilt.

For those moments when things feel less funny and more frightening, quick "What Now?" guides can be lifesavers. Let's talk emergencies that spike every dad's heart rate:

- **Choking:** If your baby suddenly can't cry or cough and looks panicked or turns blue, act fast. Turn her face down on your forearm, support her head, and give five firm pats between her shoulder blades with the heel of your hand. If she's still struggling, turn her face up and give five gentle chest compressions with two fingers just below the nipple line. Alternate until she coughs or help arrives. Call 911 right away if she doesn't respond.

- **Fever:** A rectal temperature over 100.4°F (38°C) in a newborn is an emergency. Call your pediatrician or head to the ER immediately. Don't wait it out; newborns can get sick fast.

- **Partner in Distress:** Sometimes the one who needs urgent help isn't the baby, it's your partner. Watch for signs of emotional overload: crying spells that don't stop, withdrawing from you or the baby, anger that feels out of character, or talk of hopelessness. Offer comfort and ask directly if they feel safe. If you sense it's more than exhaustion, reach out to their OB or a support line, even strong parents need backup.

Mistakes will come thick and fast in these first days, but so will victories. Maybe you finally calmed your baby after an hour-long meltdown or figured out how to change a diaper without needing a fresh shirt yourself. Perhaps you let your partner sleep an extra hour while you walked laps with your newborn pressed against your chest. Small wins like these add up. They matter more than any flawless routine. High five yourself each time you make it through a tough moment.

Here's what many new dads miss: showing up matters more than getting everything right. The wins are real, even if they're small, like holding your ground through a crying fit or making your partner laugh when both of you are running on empty. Each day you stick around, learn from mistakes, and keep going is proof that you're exactly the dad your kid needs: present, caring, and real.

CHAPTER 2

Mastering the Fundamentals: Hands-On Baby Care for Dads

The Ultimate Bottle and Breastfeeding Support Guide for Dads

I magine it's late at night: your baby's hungry, you're bleary-eyed, and the bottle warmer looks like a puzzle. Bottle and breastfeeding might seem daunting, but dads are essential to both. No matter how your baby eats, bottle, breast, or both, your support, patience, and hands-on help are invaluable.

For bottle feeds, formula, pumped milk, or both, set up a routine to make things easy when you're tired. Prep bottles by following the formula's directions precisely; even a small measurement mistake can upset your baby's stomach. Fill bottles with fresh (preferably filtered) water, add powder, shake well, and ensure lids and nipples are secure to avoid spills. Label pumped breast milk bottles clearly with the date and time. They can be kept at room temperature for up to four hours, in the fridge for up to four days, or in the freezer for up to six months. Never heat bottles in the microwave; use a bowl of warm water or a bottle warmer, and swirl gently to mix.

A dedicated "bottle station" makes a big difference. Use a section of the kitchen or a cart for bottles, nipples, formula, and burp cloths. Having extra bottles on hand saves stress on busy days. Prep for nighttime by filling bottles with water and pre-measuring scoops of formula. For twins or combo feeding, color-code or use different-shaped bottles.

If your partner breastfeeds, your role is crucial, besides producing milk! Take charge of burping: keep a cloth handy and gently pat your baby's back. Help by arranging pillows or adjusting seating for comfort. "Water and cookie runs" are classics for dads: bring snacks and drinks during long feeds. Offer encouragement over advice. Try "You're doing an amazing job" or "How can I help?" without switching to problem-solving unless asked. If your partner needs to vent, just listen and be present; sometimes sitting beside her is the best support.

For combo feeding, pace bottle feeds: hold the bottle horizontally so baby has to suck at the same pace as breastfeeding, which helps avoid confusion. Switch up who gives bottles so both parents get bonding time and rest. Many families use slow-flow nipples for a smoother transition. Test different brands if your baby fusses or rejects a bottle, as some have strong preferences.

Dads often spot feeding troubles early. Signs of a poor latch during breastfeeding include smacking sounds, lips curled inward, lots of dribbling, or pain for your partner. If you notice any of these, suggest a pause and help reposition the baby. With bottles, refusal can mean the milk is flowing too fast or too slow. Gassy babies clench their fists, arch their backs, and pull up their knees. Pace the feeds and burp often to help.

Spit-up and fussiness are common. If your baby spits up but seems content and gains weight, just keep burp cloths handy. If spit-up is forceful, greenish, or accompanied by pain or poor feeding, call your pediatrician. For fussiness, check that bottles are the right temperature, try feeding upright, or offer smaller, more frequent bottles.

Here are simple "dad hacks":

- Use dishwasher baskets so bottle parts don't vanish.
- Keep a stash of clean bottles in the fridge.
- Set phone alarms for using or freezing pumped milk.
- Gather all night-time feeding supplies before bed.
- Place burp cloths everywhere: car, couch, and changing table.

Emotional support matters as much as practical help. Feeding can bring frustration and guilt. Don't suggest formula unless your partner does; instead, say something like, "I see how hard you're working." If things get tough, remind each other you're a team and that a fed baby is what matters.

Reflection Exercise: Feeding Wins and Lessons

After each feed, jot down what worked (like a bottle your baby accepted) or a supportive word that mattered. These notes become a toolkit of what works for your family and proof that you're mastering this, one feed at a time.

Burping Without the Barf: Dad-Tested Techniques

Burping your baby is one of those rituals that quickly becomes second nature, but it can feel awkward and a little nerve-wracking at first. You'll probably find yourself cycling through different positions, trying to find the one that works best for your baby.

Over-the-shoulder is the classic move. Drape a burp cloth across your shoulder (and maybe down your back for extra coverage), then hold your baby upright with their chin resting just above your collarbone. Use one hand to support their bottom and the other to gently pat or rub their back in slow circles. This position is a favorite for a reason. It's easy, lets gravity do some of the work, and usually gets a solid burp out in record time. The downside? If your baby's going to spit up, your shirt might be collateral damage.

The sitting-on-lap method comes in handy when your back needs a break. Sit your baby on your knee facing away from you, support their chest and head with one hand (forming a "C" with your fingers under their chin), and use the other hand to pat or rub their back. This position gives you a clear view of your baby's face, so you can spot any warning signs of an impending spit-up attack.

For gassy babies who need extra help, try the face-down-on-knees trick. Lay your baby belly-down across your knees, head slightly higher than their chest, and pat or rub gently. Sometimes that change in pressure helps stubborn air bubbles escape.

Babies give plenty of hints when they need to burp; you just have to watch for them. If your little one squirms, arches their back, draws their knees up, or suddenly stops feeding and looks annoyed, there's probably a burp hiding in there. Fussiness during feeds, clenched fists, or grimacing faces are other signs it's time for a quick burp break. With bottle-fed babies, try to pause every couple of ounces to get those bubbles out before they build up. Breastfed babies may need a burp after each breast or whenever they unlatch.

Sometimes burps play hard to get. If you're patting and nothing happens after a couple of minutes, switch up the position; gravity can be your best friend. Some babies respond better to gentle rubs in a circular motion rather than firm pats. Others prefer a combination, light tapping followed by a slow upward stroke along the spine. If your baby falls asleep before you get a burp, don't panic; not every feed ends with a belch. Never force it. If your baby is relaxed and not showing signs of discomfort, it's okay to let it go.

Spit-up is almost inevitable, especially in the early weeks. When it happens, keep calm and reach for that burp cloth you wisely placed within arm's reach. Quick swaps are key. A clean cloth over your shoulder and another within grabbing distance for your baby's face or clothes can save you from needing an outfit change yourself. For especially messy spit-ups, keep an emergency onesie tucked behind the couch or in your diaper caddy for rapid response.

Dad hacks for containing the chaos? Place burp cloths everywhere: on chairs, couches, even across your lap if you're feeding in bed. Tuck an extra shirt for yourself into the diaper bag or stash one in the car for post-spit-up emergencies. During night feeds, have a "burp station" with spare cloths, wipes, and pajamas close by. You'll thank yourself when disaster strikes at 2 a.m. For quick cleanups, keep baby wipes within reach, not just for them but for you too. There's nothing like realizing you've been walking around with dried milk on your neck all day.

Normalize the mess; it's part of the new dad experience. The first time my daughter unleashed a full-on spit-up that ran down my back and pooled in my shoe, I thought I'd failed some kind of parenting test. Turns out, it happens to everyone.

One dad friend confessed he once caught spit-up in his bare hands just to save his new couch. Another dad remembered patting so vigorously during his rookie week that he ended up with a gassy but still very un-burped baby and an angry partner who'd just changed her shirt for the third time that morning.

My favorite "burp fail" happened when I tried to multitask on a work call while burping my son. He managed to spit up on both my shirt and my laptop keyboard, forcing me to finish the meeting in a bathrobe.

You'll develop "dad reflexes" faster than you think, like catching spit-up midair or swapping out a onesie in under twenty seconds flat. The key is not taking any of this too seriously; every dad has stories of disasters narrowly avoided or epic fails survived, with only minor stains as proof. Laugh off the goofs, celebrate the wins (even if they're tiny), and know that every mess cleaned up is another notch on your dad belt. The more relaxed you are about burping and its aftermath, the more confident you'll become. And trust me, your baby will pick up on that calm.

Bath Time Basics: Safety, Fun, and Dad Wins

Bathing your newborn for the first time can feel nerve-wracking. Newborns are tiny, wiggly, and can startle you with sudden cries. You might imagine peaceful bubbles, but usually, it's more like a water experiment. If you're anxious, you're not alone; many new dads worry about dropping the baby or making a mess. The important thing is: newborns do not need daily baths. Three times a week is enough, and more can dry out their skin. Until the umbilical stump falls off (usually in the first week or so), stick to sponge baths. Choose a warm, draft-free spot, like the kitchen counter, changing table, or a bed with a towel.

Gather everything beforehand: two towels, a soft washcloth, a little rinsing cup, mild baby soap, a fresh diaper, and clean clothes. Fill a basin or bowl with warm (not hot) water and check with your elbow. It should feel comfortably warm, never hot.

Lay your baby on the towel and keep most of them wrapped, exposing only one limb at a time. Wet the washcloth and start with the cleanest parts: face, then neck folds (where milk often hides), armpits, hands, and legs. Clean the diaper area last to avoid spreading germs. Use only a little soap for the scalp or hair; newborns don't get very dirty. Never leave your baby alone, even for a second. Talking or singing calms both of you; narrate what you're doing or hum a tune. Don't stress about getting it "right"; just focus on making your baby feel safe.

When you move to tub baths after the cord stump falls off, keep things simple. Use a small tub with a non-slip bottom in the sink or bathtub, and add two or three inches of warm water. Double-check the temperature with your wrist or elbow before you start. Hold your baby's head and neck with one arm and wash with the other. Some babies love the water, some will cry, but don't panic. Just stay calm and try to be quick yet gentle.

A common concern is how slippery wet babies can be. Keep a hand under their armpit and across their chest wherever possible. Have everything within reach: shampoo, soft cradle cap brush, and towels. To prevent water in the ears, gently tilt their head or use a damp washcloth rather than pouring water. Tears are normal at first, especially if your baby is hungry or tired. Move efficiently, then wrap your baby in a hooded towel and snuggle them dry.

Bath time accidents are normal. Expect some splashing or the classic surprise pee mid-bath. You might drop the soap or fumble a towel. Stay light-hearted; every dad goes through these moments. Soon, you'll figure out what works best. Maybe soft background music or letting your baby hold a little washcloth helps them relax.

Bath time isn't just about cleaning, it's prime dad-bonding time. The first time I bathed my son solo, he screamed as soon as his foot touched water. I started singing "Rubber Duckie," and to my relief, he paused, letting me finish. I snapped a selfie afterward as proof I survived. If you want to mark these moments, take a photo, calm or not; a wild hair shot is priceless. Make a ritual with a regular song or silly saying; over time, your child will expect it and may even laugh.

As your baby grows, a soft bath toy or rubber duck can distract them. Keep baths brief; five to ten minutes is enough. Dry well between skin folds to prevent irritation.

Celebrate little milestones, like the first splash or the first time your baby reaches for the water.

Bathing your baby isn't about perfection; it's about patience and care as you learn together. Every bath builds your confidence and your baby's trust. Those are the real wins.

Diaper Blowouts: Prevention, Cleanup, and Staying Cool

Diaper blowouts are a common, humbling part of parenting, especially in the early weeks when babies are on liquid diets and their digestive systems are unpredictable. Many think blowouts are just bad luck, but in reality, proper fit and timing matter a lot. If a diaper is too loose at the legs or too small for your baby's growing belly, leaks are inevitable.

To make sure the fit is right, check the snugness at the waist (below the belly button), look for no gaping at the thighs, and make sure the tabs are evenly fastened. Red marks mean it's too tight; gaps or sagging mean it's too big. Always size by weight, not age, and refer to the manufacturer's guide on the diaper pack. Sometimes a particular brand just won't suit your baby's shape, so don't hesitate to try a few before settling on the right one.

When a blowout happens, and it will eventually, your mission is to keep the mess from spreading. The key tool is the "blowout kit": pack a couple of diapers, travel wipes, a soft cloth, a change of clothes for the baby (and maybe for yourself), and two plastic bags (one for dirty items, one for used wipes and diapers). Keep a kit everywhere you might need it: in the diaper bag, car, stroller, and by your main changing area at home.

When you spot a blowout, like stains creeping up the back or down the legs, act quickly. Lay your baby on a wipeable surface (avoid soft furnishings), roll the onesie down using the shoulder "envelopes" to avoid getting the mess in their hair, and use plenty of wipes or give a quick rinse in the tub if needed. Seal dirty clothes and diapers in a bag, take a deep breath, and remind yourself you handled it like a pro.

Preparation and speed are crucial. Keep old towels or puppy pads handy for backup changing surfaces. If a blowout hits furniture, blot with wipes, then use a safe disinfectant spray. Avoid scrubbing to prevent deep stains. In public, use family bathrooms when you can, or turn your car's trunk into a makeshift changing area. If needed, open both rear doors on your car for some privacy. Never change a baby on restaurant tables; people remember that move.

Nighttime blowouts are especially tough when you're tired and slow to react. Having pajamas and wipes within reach makes things easier. Some use double-diapering at night (a larger diaper over the normal one) if their baby is especially prone to leaks.

Dad strategies make a huge difference when you're facing blowouts. Pre-pack several diaper bags: keep one in the car, one by the door, and one attached to the stroller. Always include at least two changes of baby clothes (one won't cut it), and maybe a spare shirt for yourself. For public incidents, create a "containment zone" with extra mats or disposable liners. If things go south, just get the job done, protect your dignity, and move on with a sense of humor.

Most dads have a blowout horror story. For some, it's the back-and-leg coverage at a picnic; for others, it's a 3 a.m. mess where they wear as much as the baby. The truth is, no one gets it right every time, but you get faster and calmer with each one. After a few blowouts, you become unfazed. Grab your kit, protect the surroundings, and act.

Ultimately, what matters isn't your cleaning speed or stain removal skills, but your attitude when things go wrong. Embarrassment vanishes when you realize it's a universal dad experience. Laugh at yourself, forget about ruined clothes, and push ahead. Blowouts remind you that, despite the chaos, your presence and willingness to handle the mess are most important, even if you smell like wipes and baby powder afterwards.

Safe Sleep Without Swaddling: What Works Now

The rules for safe baby sleep have changed a lot over the years, and if you're like me, you probably heard all sorts of advice from grandparents, friends, or even your own parents about wrapping your baby up tight. But here's the honest truth: swaddling isn't considered the go-to answer anymore. The main reason is safety. Once babies get strong enough to roll, even a little, a swaddle can become a hazard if it slips or the baby ends up face down. The American Academy of Pediatrics now recommends ditching swaddles as soon as your baby shows any signs of rolling over. Instead, you want your baby to sleep on their back, always, on a firm mattress with a fitted sheet only. No bumpers, pillows, stuffed animals, or loose blankets in the crib. It might look a little bare, but that's exactly how it should be. Minimal is best for safe sleep.

So what do you do when your baby startles awake or fusses without that tight swaddle? Enter the hero of modern sleep: the sleep sack. These wearable blankets keep babies warm without any loose fabric in the crib. There are tons of options; some with arms out, some with gentle snugness around the torso but freedom for the legs. Layer your baby in a onesie and footed pajamas under the sleep sack for chilly nights. If you're worried about them getting cold, remember: one more layer than you're wearing is usually plenty.

White noise machines can work wonders too. Steady sounds help block out household noise and mimic the whoosh babies heard in the womb. Place the machine near the crib but away from your baby's head, and keep it at a low volume. Pacifiers are also recommended for safe sleep after breastfeeding is established; they can soothe and reduce the risk of SIDS.

A pre-sleep routine is gold for signaling "bedtime" to your baby's little brain. This doesn't have to be complicated. Dim the lights, put on soft music or white noise, and move slowly through diaper changes and pajamas. A gentle rocking session or soft singing can help your baby wind down. Try the same steps each night; babies catch on quickly when there's a predictable pattern. You'll notice them yawning or rubbing their eyes when they sense bedtime coming.

Even with all these tools, you'll probably run into challenges like startle reflexes; those sudden flailing arms that wake your baby just as you tiptoe out of the room. Startle reflex is normal and fades with age, but it can be tough in those early weeks. Sleep sacks with snug upper bodies help keep arms in check without restricting movement dangerously. Layering for warmth is another trick; sometimes a well-fitted onesie and cozy sack can make your baby feel secure enough to settle back down.

If your baby wakes often or fights sleep, try holding them upright and gently rocking side to side, not up and down, for a few minutes before putting them back down drowsy but awake.

Night wakings are part of the deal, especially early on, but there are ways to make them less brutal. Tag-team with your partner if possible; split shifts or alternate who gets up each time so neither of you burns out completely. If you're solo, set up everything you might need (diapers, wipes, bottle/supplies) within arm's reach of the crib before you go to bed. Keep lights low during wake-ups so your baby knows it's still "sleep time," not playtime.

Tracking your baby's sleep doesn't have to be complicated; a simple log helps spot patterns and celebrate progress. Use a notebook or a phone app to jot down when your baby goes down and wakes up, plus notes on what helped (or didn't). You'll start to see trends: maybe she does longer stretches after a warm bath or fusses less with white noise on. It's so easy to miss progress when you're exhausted, but looking back at your notes and seeing "first three-hour stretch!" or "self-soothed at 2 a.m." can give you a boost when you need it most.

Those small victories, when your baby sleeps through a diaper change without waking fully, or finally soothes herself with a pacifier, are wins worth celebrating. Maybe you get an extra hour of shut-eye, or you high-five your partner at 5 a.m. after surviving another night shift. These moments add up; each one builds confidence and proves you're figuring this out together, one night at a time.

Sleep Log Template

Just jot this in your phone notes or on a sticky by the crib:

- Down time:
- Wake time:
- How long they slept:
- What helped them settle:
- Any "win" (like longer stretch or less fuss): Seeing those wins, even tiny ones, reminds you this stage won't last forever, and you're doing better than you think.

Taming the Witching Hour: Soothing Strategies for Fussy Evenings

Every new dad gets hit with the "witching hour" at some point, and it's a wild ride. Picture this: the sun's gone down, you're wiped, and suddenly your calm baby turns into a tiny, red-faced siren. Usually, this madness kicks off between five and eight in the evening. It's almost like your baby's internal alarm clock is set to "maximum chaos" right when you're hoping for a breather.

If you're staring at your child, wondering why nothing calms them, you're in good company. This is the time of day when babies often get overstimulated, overtired, or just plain cranky from all the new sights and sounds piling up. Hunger sneaks in too, even if you fed them an hour ago. Sometimes, it's just their way of letting off steam. There isn't always a clear reason, but there are plenty of ways dads can get ahead of it.

The best defense is to anticipate the storm. Notice if your baby starts yawning, rubbing eyes, or gets extra clingy in the early evening. These are signs it's almost witching hour. If you can catch these cues early, sometimes a quick feed or nap can help head off a meltdown. Set the mood: lower the lights around the house, mute the TV, and keep stimulation to a minimum. Babies pick up on your energy. If you start moving slower and talking softer, they often follow suit.

When things kick off, you need a toolbox of soothing moves. Babywearing is my favorite. Strap your kid in a carrier and start pacing the living room or stroll outside if the weather permits. The rhythm of your walk plus your body heat often settles even the fussiest little one.

The "5 S's" from pediatrician Harvey Karp are legendary for a reason: shushing (loud enough to match their cries), swinging (gentle sways or bouncing on an exercise ball), sucking (pacifier or clean finger), side or stomach holding (only while you're watching them, never for sleep), and swaddling alternatives like sleep sacks if they're still under four months and not rolling. Though swaddling isn't the long-term answer, a snug sleep sack or your arms can create comfort without risk.

Turn on white noise; apps, fans, or dedicated machines all work. This background hum drowns out jarring household sounds and gives babies something steady to focus on. If you can't find a white noise machine fast enough, try running water in the bathroom or even softly humming yourself. Don't underestimate the "dad dance" either. A silly two-step in the kitchen or slow swaying with music can transform hysteria into giggles (or at least a quieter cry).

Keeping your sanity as a dad is just as important as soothing your baby. Tag-team with your partner: swap every twenty minutes so nobody feels like they're losing their mind. Prep easy dinners ahead, like frozen pizzas or slow cooker meals, so you don't add hunger to the stress mix.

Humor is a secret weapon; go ahead and narrate your baby's meltdown like a sports commentator or make faces until one of you cracks up. Playlists help too. Create one of calming music for your baby and one for yourself (sometimes punk rock is therapy). Podcasts are great for keeping your brain occupied while you rock endlessly.

Supporting your partner can turn a rough night into teamwork instead of tension. Don't try to fix everything; sometimes all they want is a nod and a "this sucks, but we've got this." A simple "want me to take over for a bit?" goes a long way. Knowing when to step in and when to offer space makes a huge difference.

Real stories make this real. I remember one dad who only survived those hours by doing laps around his kitchen with his son in a carrier while listening to jazz. He swears it was the trumpet solos that did the trick. Another friend tried every trick he could find online before realizing his daughter just wanted to be held skin-to-skin on his chest while he watched old baseball highlights. Sometimes what works one day flops the next; flexibility is key.

Here are some top dad-approved moves:

1. Walks outside with baby in a carrier
2. White noise on repeat
3. Low lights and soft talking
4. "Dad dance" routines with calming music
5. Calling in backup when patience runs out

There will be evenings when nothing seems to work. That doesn't mean you're failing; it just means your baby is being a baby. Some problems don't have instant fixes. Trust that being present and calm (or faking calm) actually does help your child, even if they're still crying.

To wrap up this chapter: every dad faces rough nights, but each one teaches you something new about your baby, and probably yourself. You'll build skills and patience you never knew you had, and even on the loudest nights, you're forging the bond that matters most. Next up, we'll dig into building connections with your little one every single month because it's not just about surviving, it's about growing together.

CHAPTER 3

Building Bonds: Dad and Baby Connection Month by Month

The Science and Art of Dad-Baby Bonding

Picture this: You're sitting on the couch, baby in your lap, both of you blinking under the glow of a late-night lamp. Maybe your newborn stares past your shoulder, maybe they yawn, or maybe they're just a warm little bundle snoozing on your chest. You might wonder, *"Is this what bonding is supposed to feel like?"*

Here's the thing: bonding doesn't always arrive with fireworks or movie-moment music. For some dads, it's instant. For others, it's slow, built through repetition, touch, and those quiet little moments when the world seems to pause and the only thing that matters is the person in your arms.

Let's break down what actually happens in your body and mind as you get to know your baby. Modern science

49

confirms that you, as a dad, are not just a bystander to this experience. When you spend time holding, talking to, and caring for your baby, your brain chemistry shifts. Your body ramps up production of oxytocin, the so-called "love hormone." This isn't just a buzzword; oxytocin actually helps you feel calmer and more connected to your child. Prolactin, another hormone often linked with nurturing behavior, rises as well, especially after hands-on care or soothing routines. These changes aren't exclusive to moms; dads experience them too, especially with regular physical closeness and involvement.

It goes even deeper. Every time you hold your baby, make eye contact, or even just talk in that goofy "dad voice," you're sending signals that help wire their developing brain. Early touch, gentle pats, cuddles, or resting your baby against your chest—stimulates neural pathways crucial for emotional and sensory growth. Your voice becomes a familiar soundscape for your baby's world; studies show that hearing dad's voice regularly can help build language skills and emotional security. Presence isn't about doing everything perfectly; it's about showing up again and again, making your baby feel safe and known.

There's a myth out there that bonding is automatic, or that moms have some secret advantage dads can never match. It's just not true. Sure, some parents feel an immediate connection, but many need more time. Maybe you're still waiting for that "aha" moment when the rush of love hits. Maybe you're worried because you haven't had one yet. That's normal. Research shows that many dads grow their bond through daily routines, bathing, diaper changes, reading stories, even if it starts out feeling awkward or forced. In fact, studies estimate upwards of 60% of dads describe their strongest connection forming during the everyday grind rather than magical first encounters.

The long-term benefits of early bonding show up in both you and your child. Kids with a strong attachment to their fathers tend to be more emotionally resilient. They bounce back from stress faster and show more curiosity about the world around them. These children usually develop richer vocabularies and better social skills by the time they reach school age. For dads, the payoff is real: those who bond early report less stress overall and greater confidence in their parenting abilities. Feeling connected also helps buffer against anxiety and makes it easier to ride out the tough nights or tantrum days.

If you're finding it tough to connect right now, you're not alone. I've talked to dads who said they felt more like a bodyguard than a parent at first, guarding naps, guarding peace and quiet, but not really feeling that spark. One dad told me it took three months before he felt anything beyond basic responsibility; another admitted he didn't feel "like a real dad" until his baby smiled at him for the first time. There's no deadline for bonding; what matters is showing up and trying.

Reflection Exercise: Finding Your Bond

Grab a notebook or open your phone notes tonight after the baby goes down. Write out one thing, no matter how small, that made you feel close or at least present for your child today. Did you like the way their hand curled around your finger? Did they react to your goofy face or settle when you hummed a tune?

If nothing jumps out yet, jot down what you hope will help you connect: a walk together, reading aloud, or just narrating what you're doing as you hold them. Try this every few days. Looking back in a month or two, you'll see patterns form and probably notice moments of connection that felt invisible in real time.

Bonding isn't a contest or a test. It's a process made up of millions of tiny interactions stacked together over days and weeks. You're building something lasting each time you pause to listen, hold, or simply be there, even if you're also half-asleep or wondering what comes next. You've got more instincts than you think, and every day brings another chance to find your own way into this relationship.

Hands-On From Day One: Skin-to-Skin and Beyond

Picture yourself shirtless, your baby resting against your bare chest while you both breathe quietly. This is skin-to-skin contact. It's simple but deeply meaningful. Start by finding a private, warm spot, whether it's a hospital room, your bedroom, or a living room chair. Silence your phone, turn off distractions, and ensure the room is cozy for your undressed baby. Place your baby on your chest, cover you both with a blanket to retain warmth, and support their back and neck. Let your heartbeat soothe them. Skin-to-skin isn't limited to those first hours; it's equally valuable during hospital recovery, after baths, or during peaceful moments at home. Let your baby rest or move as long as you're both comfortable.

The golden hour after birth is ideal for skin-to-skin, but any time, hospital stay, at home, morning, or night, works. Those first days are hectic, but even ten minutes of this connection matters. If you missed skin-to-skin immediately post-birth, don't worry; it's never too late to start.

Physical bonding continues beyond the newborn phase. Babywearing is an excellent way to maintain closeness. Use a soft carrier or sling to keep your baby near as you go about your day, letting them enjoy your movement, scent, and voice. Walk around the block or gently move as you tidy up. Infant massage is another powerful bonding tool: gently massage their arms, legs, and back with baby-safe oil after a bath or before bed. This can calm fussy babies and strengthen your bond. Day-to-day playful touch, raspberries on tummies, lifting games, and gentle tickles also deepens your connection and makes routine moments special.

Feeling awkward is common. When I first tried skin-to-skin with my daughter, I felt exposed and uncertain, especially in the hospital. My daughter squirmed; I doubted whether I was doing it "right." Other dads have similar worries, concerns about body hair, privacy, or feeling out of place. But after a few minutes, it often clicks: your baby's warmth calms you, and self-consciousness fades. If you feel nervous, try deep breathing or humming, focusing on the simple comfort between you and your child. There's no performance or right way, just real connection.

Many dads miss the immediate post-birth bonding window due to adoption, C-sections, NICU stays, or chaotic deliveries. Skin-to-skin is for every family, no matter the timing. Adoptive or non-birthing dads should start whenever possible, even weeks after birth. For NICU babies, kangaroo care (holding your diapered baby upright against your chest under a blanket) is incredibly valuable. Nurses can help arrange safe positions if your newborn has wires or monitors; don't hesitate to ask.

If you're anxious about looking awkward or making mistakes, realize every dad feels that way at first. Don't let nervousness stop you. Prepare your space in advance to avoid scrambling while holding your baby. If privacy is a concern, have your partner or nurse give you time alone. If your baby fusses initially, that's normal. Try again later, perhaps after a feed when they're calm.

Skin-to-skin adapts to all situations. If you can't be present (travel, deployment), have your partner use a blanket with your scent during baby cuddles. For adoption or surrogacy, begin skin-to-skin as soon as you're allowed. It immediately fosters attachment.

Interactive Exercise: Skin-To-Skin Confidence Builder

Set aside 10–20 minutes for skin-to-skin with your baby. Eliminate distractions, hold them close, and focus on their breathing and movements. After, jot down three words describing your feelings: awkward, peaceful, proud, sleepy, or anything else. Repeat weekly to see how your comfort and connection evolve.

Remember, skin-to-skin isn't about perfect technique. It's about being there, physically and emotionally, for your child, no matter how uncertain or clumsy it may feel at first.

Bonding Without Feeding: Creative
Involvement for All Dads

Sometimes you end up feeling like a third wheel during feeding sessions, especially in those early months if your partner is breastfeeding or pumping. It's normal to wonder where you fit in when the spotlight keeps swinging away. But here's the secret: some of the strongest dad-baby bonds aren't built with a bottle or breast, but through the everyday routines you shape together. One of the simplest ways to carve out your own space is by taking charge of the morning routine. Start each day with a "dad greeting." Pick your own ritual, whether it's a silly song, a gentle stretch with your baby on your lap, or just opening the curtains and narrating what you see outside. Babies thrive on predictability, and your face, voice, and touch become anchor points in their day. If your child is already at the age where they're alert and responsive in the morning, make it your time for one-on-one giggles, mirror play, or even just a quiet cuddle while you sip your coffee. This becomes your thing, and it matters.

Bedtime is another golden opportunity. While feeding might be part of the pre-sleep routine, there's always room for a dad-only ritual. You can lead bath time and turn it into a comedy set: think rubber duck races and goofy bath time jokes, or claim storytime as your personal stage. Even if your baby can't follow the words yet, your voice and presence help them wind down. Make up a personalized lullaby (it doesn't have to rhyme), or pick a favorite book to read every night. Some dads invent bedtime "call-and-response" games. Maybe you say, "Goodnight toes!" and your baby wiggles their feet, or you count stuffed animals together before lights out. The trick is consistency; babies love knowing what comes next, and before long, these moments belong to both of you.

Want to be the king of tummy time? Set up play mat sessions with high-contrast toys or just stretch out next to your baby, talking about everything you see. Make silly faces, narrate your movements, or introduce simple games like "airplane arms" or tapping out rhythms on the mat. These sessions build strength for your baby and confidence for you. If you're feeling unsure what to say or do, just describe what's happening ("You're pushing up so strong!") or sing your favorite childhood song. If you're up for it, get down on their level and let them touch your beard, glasses, or fingers. Babies are fascinated by their dads' features.

Feeling left out during marathon nursing or pumping sessions happens to almost every dad. Instead of sitting in the background scrolling your phone, look for ways to redirect that energy into another connection point. Offer to burp the baby after feeds, change diapers right after, or plan a mini-adventure once feeding ends, maybe a lap around the house or stepping out on the porch for some fresh air together. If direct involvement feels impossible in those moments, prep something special for later, a playlist of calming tunes for bedtime, a silly hat for tomorrow's playtime, or even just laying out a fresh onesie with a note for your partner.

Scripts and rituals help make these routines stick. Try announcing bedtime with a "Dad's sleepy song" or inventing a morning cheer ("Rise and shine with Daddy time!"). Start bath time with a classic dad joke, corny puns are welcome here ("Why did the duck cross the tub? To get to the other tide!"). You might even invent your own gentle handshake or foot wiggle routine before putting on pajamas. The important thing is repetition; even if it feels goofy at first, your baby will start to anticipate these moments and respond in their own way.

To keep things fresh and challenge yourself as a new dad, give yourself mini-goals each week. Try the "one-on-one adventure" challenge: take your baby on a solo walk around the block (weather permitting), introduce them to new sounds in the backyard, or create an indoor scavenger hunt for soft toys. Another week, focus on low-key sensory games. Sit together in front of a mirror and mimic each other's faces, crinkle paper for sound exploration, or gently blow raspberries on their tummy to see if you can coax a giggle. Mark down any new reaction or skill you notice; these are signs your relationship is growing.

It's easy to get discouraged if you feel sidelined from feeding or if bonding doesn't happen overnight. The truth is that every dad has days when they feel like an extra in their own home movie. The key is persistence and creativity, finding rhythms that work for you and your child, even if they look nothing like what you imagined. Give yourself credit for showing up and experimenting; every routine you create becomes another thread in the fabric of your relationship with your child.

Dad-and-Baby Adventures: Month-by-Month Activity Guides

The first year with your baby is packed with newness. Every single month brings a different little person to your arms. Kicking things off in month one, you'll find your baby's world is small and their needs are simple. Gentle walks become golden. Wrap your baby snug in a carrier, step out into the air, and narrate the world as you stroll. Point out the neighbor's barking dog, the crunch of leaves, or the rhythm of rain on the sidewalk. Even if they sleep through it, the sound of your voice and the steady movement builds comfort.

Back at home, soft music, anything from jazz to lullabies, can fill the background as you rock together, creating a shared playlist of calm. Don't underestimate how even just lying together with your baby on your chest, breathing in sync, can be an adventure for both of you.

Three months in, your baby is getting more alert, and this is when play takes on a new meaning. Tummy time moves from being a battle to a game. Lay out a high-contrast mat or even a bold-patterned towel, and get down on their level.

61

Make silly faces, mimic their little noises, wiggle a toy just out of reach. This is when you might see that first real grin just for you, a milestone all its own. Add in high-contrast toys, a black-and-white picture book, or even just a shiny kitchen spoon for entertainment. The goal isn't fancy gear but giving your baby's eyes and brain something to explore while you're right there cheering them on.

By six months, things ramp up again. It's peekaboo season. Babies start to understand object permanence, so covering your face with your hands and popping out with a goofy smile gets big laughs. Supported sitting opens up a new world: prop your baby with pillows and sit facing them, rolling a soft ball back and forth or clapping together to music. The weather's warming up? Take the stroller outside for longer rides. Narrate everything, talk about birds overhead, describe the smells of grass or a neighbor's barbecue drifting by. Even quick trips to the mailbox turn into an expedition if you keep up a running commentary.

At nine months, babies move fast. Crawling races across a rug or grass patch can turn a grumpy afternoon into giggles. Set up sensory bins, fill a shallow tub with safe objects like silicone spatulas, soft cloths, or textured toys, and let them explore as you talk about what they're touching. Crank up the music for "dad dance parties." Hold your baby tight or let them bop in your lap while you groove. They'll love the movement and your uninhibited silliness.

Twelve months brings new horizons. Your child is ready for their first playground adventure. Even if they're not walking solo yet, swings and slides (with your help) are pure joy. Try simple hide-and-seek behind trees or playground equipment; those peals of laughter will stick with you for years. Chase them around on all fours if they're crawling or tottering; they'll think you're hilarious.

Routine chores don't have to be boring for either of you. Turn grocery shopping into a scavenger hunt by pointing out colors, naming fruits, or letting them hold a (soft) item in the cart. Folding laundry? Narrate each step, "Here's Dad's blue sock! Where's yours?", and see if they'll help crumple shirts or toss socks into piles. These simple activities make everyday tasks feel like little games and strengthen your connection.

Dad adventures aren't just fun; they shape your baby's confidence and curiosity while giving you purpose beyond the daily grind. Each outing, no matter how small, helps them feel safe exploring the world with you nearby. You'll notice them scanning for your reaction when something new happens; they trust your cues on what's exciting or safe. As these routines become familiar, you'll see their eyes light up when you pull out their favorite book or get ready for another stroller ride.

Growth isn't just measured in inches or milestones; it lives in these moments when you both step outside your comfort zones together. Documenting these adventures adds another layer of meaning. Try jotting down monthly "dad win" journal entries, a quick note on what made you proud or laugh that month, even if it was just surviving a meltdown at Target without losing your marbles. Snap photos during outings or at home, messy breakfast faces, wild hair after bath time, that first trip down the slide, and turn them into a "first year with dad" photo collage for your wall or phone background.

Looking back at these memories, you'll realize how much you've both changed, and how many stories you've collected together along the way.

Handling Baby's Preference for the Other Parent

Many dads experience moments when their baby seems fixated on someone else, usually their partner. You might reach out, but your baby twists away or cries for mom. It stings and raises questions about your parenting, but this preference is normal and usually about familiarity, routine, and comfort. Babies bond most with the person who is around most often or provides primary care, especially between six and nine months, when separation anxiety develops and your baby learns you and your partner are truly separate people. While it feels personal, it's not a judgment on your abilities or love.

To stay connected, you need intention and creativity. Rather than withdrawing (even though it's tempting), create routines that build your relationship. Try getting up early for solo morning snuggles, even if it's only fifteen minutes of quiet rocking, or take over bath time once or twice a week and make it playful. When your partner is out, don't just see it as babysitting; take the opportunity to confidently engage: carry your baby while doing chores, narrate what you're doing, or sing a "dad song" that becomes your own ritual.

Consistency is what matters. Even if your baby fusses for mom, persist with your routines. Over time, they'll become predictable and comforting.

Avoid letting resentment creep in by communicating openly with your partner. Establish and stick to routines so both of you know when you'll each have one-on-one time with your baby. If your child reaches for the other parent during a difficult moment, gently reassure your baby but don't immediately give in; finish the task and say, "Dad's here right now," with quiet confidence. This helps avoid undermining one another or competing for affection. Debrief together later about what's working or if anyone needs extra support.

Stories from other dads offer perspective during these phases. One father found himself always the "backup parent," and every attempt to soothe his son was met with crying for mom. However, he kept going: daily walks, goofy bath routines, a unique dad peekaboo voice. One day, with mom gone and his son upset after a nap, he picked him up expecting resistance, but the boy calmed down and cuddled in. That was the turning point, and after that, bedtime stories became their thing. Another dad shared that his daughter preferred mom for months, until a weekend road trip forced six hours of solo time together. After that, she reached happily for him at home, showing how patience and consistent presence pay off.

These phases can shift without warning. One week you're ignored; the next, you're the hero who gets the giggle or calms teething tears. Babies don't tally the days; they remember the presence and persistence. When frustration builds (and it will), remember this doesn't last forever. Your consistent effort forms the bonds your child will rely on as they grow.

Staying involved means showing up even when it's tough. Don't wait for an invitation; carve out solo moments and treat them as opportunities, not pass-fail tests. Sometimes connection builds during unexpected times, a giggle at a chaotic diaper change or a quiet moment during a walk. These memories create trust and comfort that outlast any phase or temporary preference.

Working as a team with your partner strengthens your family and benefits your child. When both parents stick to routines and support each other in front of the baby, you send the message that both of you are safe and reliable. If you haven't had that moment of being chosen yet, keep showing up. Eventually, those little arms will reach for you, and when that happens, all your patience will be worth it.

Spotlight Stories: Connection Wins from Diverse Dads

Real connection with your child doesn't come with instructions, and every dad finds his own way. From talking with other dads, it's obvious there are countless ways to build meaningful bonds, no matter your background or family setup. Take Marcus, a single dad who adopted his son after years of waiting. On adoption day, he began drawing tiny smiley faces on his son's toes, a simple ritual that became their cherished "thing." Each morning, despite any chaos, Marcus would doodle a face, inventing funny stories about those toes. It created a lighthearted moment for both and gave his son something to look forward to each day.

Owen co-parents with his husband, and their daughter joined them after a tough NICU stay. Feeling overwhelmed and out of place, Owen started "Superhero Story Hour." Instead of just reading, he invented tales where their daughter was the hero, building rockets from pillows or outsmarting dragons. This ritual made bedtime fun, helped them bond as a family, and created a sense of team spirit. James, another dad, lives with a physical disability, making some activities difficult. Rather than focus on what he couldn't do, he embraced his strengths, like voice acting. Every bath became a "radio show," with James voicing pirates or undersea adventurers. Bath time became a highlight, showing that connection comes from energy and intention, not just physical activity.

These rituals don't have to be elaborate. A dad started a "Daddy-Daughter Breakfast Club" at the local diner every Saturday, just him, his toddler, and animal-shaped pancakes. That simple routine became their special time to bond. Another friend snapped a selfie before every morning walk with his son, creating a growing timeline of their relationship. Secret handshakes, silly dances during commercials, or a special shoulder tap before bed: all these routines become anchors in a child's memory. It doesn't matter if you parent solo, with a partner, or in a blended family; traditions are yours to create.

What stands out is that creativity matters more than perfection. Keep experimenting until you find your "signature move," the thing your kid will remember as uniquely "dad." Maybe it's a made-up diaper-changing song, a dance before nap, or something else entirely. The first attempt may be awkward, but kids love repetition and will show you what they enjoy.

If you're not sure where to begin, pick a routine part of the day, like getting dressed or cleaning up, and make it playful. Narrate it like a sports game, or challenge your child to a funny face contest. As you get more comfortable and your child engages, these small moments can become the best part of your day.

If you worry your bond isn't strong because of work, shared custody, or nerves, let these stories reassure you. Every dad brings something unique. All kids need are small, consistent signals that say, "I want to spend time with you." Whether it's ten minutes at bedtime or an hour on weekends, the more you show up, the stronger your connection will be.

Celebrate Your Win

Pause tonight and notice a moment that went right, a smile at storytime, a giggle at breakfast, a hug as you buckle your child in. Mark it in your mind or jot it down. It doesn't have to be big, just real and yours. If you like, start a "connection wins" list: each week, record one moment when you felt truly present with your child. Over time, you'll see just how many wins you have.

There is no single way to be "the connected dad." It's about being open, trying, and showing up in ways that feel right for your family. Whether it's superhero tales or weekend pancakes, your presence is what counts.

Connection isn't built on grand gestures; it's found in small rituals, silly smiles, and daily habits you make your own. As we finish this chapter on building bonds, remember: little moments matter most. Next, we'll dig into supporting your partner, because being a great dad also means being there for the whole family.

CHAPTER 4

Supporting Your Partner: Postpartum, Teamwork, and Real Talk

Recognizing and Responding to Postpartum Mood Changes

Bringing home your baby might feel like entering a new world. One full of exhaustion and chaos, but also unpredictable mood swings. You may find yourself unsure how to respond as your partner's emotions shift dramatically from laughter to tears. One friend likened it to a house of mirrors, never quite knowing who you'll encounter next. This invisible, emotional rollercoaster is a typical part of the early postpartum period. While sometimes it's just temporary "baby blues," other times it's more serious. Your support as a new dad truly matters.

Almost all new moms experience postpartum blues, a wave of mood swings, irritability, anxiety, sadness, and crying that appears within days of birth and may last a few weeks. These mood changes come without much warning. Your partner may shift from lovingly watching over your baby to being upset about something minor. This is normal: her body is recovering, and hormones are fluctuating wildly. Usually, baby blues don't get in the way of her caring for your baby or you, and there are still moments of brightness.

However, sometimes these feelings don't subside, becoming more persistent and disruptive; this is postpartum depression (PPD). Unlike the blues, PPD stays for weeks or even months and can involve a range of symptoms. Your partner might start withdrawing from you or the baby, passing off care tasks, or avoiding affection and citing the need for space. You might notice ongoing, intense crying, uncharacteristic anger, or restlessness that doesn't ease with sleep.

Other signs include insomnia even when the baby sleeps, spacing out during conversation, loss of appetite, binge eating, headaches, or panic attacks. Listen carefully if she voices doubts about being a good mom or expresses hopelessness. There's also postpartum anxiety, racing thoughts, and constant worry that something may happen to the baby. Very rarely, postpartum psychosis can occur, including confusion or hallucinations—a medical emergency that requires immediate attention.

What can you do? Trust your instincts; you know your partner best. If you sense something is wrong, don't wait. Approach with empathy, not judgment. Avoid dismissive advice like "Just get some sleep." Instead, try: "I've noticed you seem down this week, do you want to talk?" or "It looks like you're having a tough time lately; I'm here for you." You don't have to solve the problem, just let her know she's not alone. If she's not ready to talk, just being there speaks volumes.

Active listening is crucial now. Eliminate distractions and give her your full attention. Use reflective listening: "So you're feeling overwhelmed every night when it gets dark?" Unless she asks, don't offer fixes. Just listening can ease her burden.

If symptoms persist over two weeks or intensify, seek outside help. It might feel uncomfortable to suggest therapy or professional support, but frame it gently: "I care about you and want us to be strong for our baby. I think talking to someone could help." Offer to help find a therapist or be there for the first call or appointment. If therapy feels too daunting, suggest talking with a trusted friend or family member. Build a ready list of resources such as postpartum support groups, mental health hotlines, or online communities.

Interactive Element: Quick Mood Change Checklist for Dads

- Has my partner withdrawn from me or our baby?
- Is she crying excessively or showing unexplained anger?
- Is she unable to sleep, even when exhausted?
- Any sudden appetite changes?
- Is she feeling hopeless or like a "bad mom"?
- Signs of panic attacks: racing heart, dizziness, shaking?
- Any mention of seeing or hearing things that aren't real?

Check more than two boxes (especially if symptoms last more than two weeks)? Reach out for professional support.

Supporting your partner during postpartum mood swings isn't about fixing everything; it's about being present, listening, and knowing when to get help so your family can move forward.

The Partner Support Playbook: Small Actions, Big Impact

There's no medal for "Most Helpful Dad," but if there were, it would go to the guy who steps in before anyone asks. The biggest difference you can make isn't about grand gestures; it's the little things done every day. You start by scanning the room: dishes piling up, laundry basket overflowing, trash can threatening to erupt. Instead of waiting for a nudge, you roll up your sleeves and get to work.

Taking on chores without being asked isn't about earning points; it's about showing that you're in this together. You empty the dishwasher while your partner feeds the baby. You wipe down counters and prep the next round of bottles while she catches her breath. On days when she's glued to the couch feeding or pumping, a glass of water and a snack tray within reach is a lifeline. It's these unsung acts, refilling her water before she asks, making sure there's fresh fruit or a granola bar nearby, that say "I see you, I've got you."

Managing visitors is its own level of support. Friends and family mean well, but their timing can be less than ideal. You become the gatekeeper, texting back, "Now's not great, but we'll let you know when we're ready for company." Sometimes you have to be direct, setting boundaries so your partner isn't stuck making small talk when she'd rather nap or just exist in stretchy pants. Protecting her space is an invisible shield she'll never forget.

Anticipating needs is almost like learning a new language; one spoken with raised eyebrows, weary sighs, or silence. Maybe you notice she's gone quiet or her eyelids droop in the afternoon light. Instead of asking, "Do you want to rest?" you scoop up the baby and say, "I'm heading out for a walk, take a nap." You run the bathwater without waiting for a request, light a candle, and usher her in for twenty minutes of quiet while you handle the chaos outside the door. Sometimes it's as simple as taking over baby duty so she can eat with both hands or shower without the soundtrack of newborn cries.

Invisible labor is everywhere, lists in your partner's head you probably never see. She tracks feeding schedules, doctor appointments, when to order more diapers, and if there's enough formula on hand for tomorrow. You step up by grabbing your phone and setting reminders for pediatrician visits or updating the shared calendar with vaccine appointments. You keep an eye on baby supplies and reorder before things run low. If your fridge looks sad or the pantry shelf is bare, you build a quick grocery list and hit the store, or order delivery if that's all you've got in you. Organizing meals takes stress off her plate; maybe you set up a meal train with friends or batch-cook simple dinners to stash in the freezer.

Real-life stories drive this home. One mom told me her husband left a sticky note on the bathroom mirror every Monday: "You're tougher than you think." Another dad ran out to buy her favorite ice cream at 10 p.m., no special reason other than he remembered she'd mentioned craving it days ago. A friend described how her partner started keeping a shared to-do list on their phones; whenever he finished something (restocked wipes, paid a bill), he marked it off without being prompted. It sounds small, but seeing those tasks disappear made her feel less alone.

Encouragement often comes in quiet moments, like slipping an "I love you" note into her robe pocket or texting a silly meme when she's stuck under a sleeping baby. Sometimes it's running interference with that one well-meaning aunt who always overstays ("We're heading to nap time now, let's catch up another day"). Other times it's about action, like taking over nighttime rocking so your partner can get two uninterrupted hours of sleep.

A shared to-do list, physical or digital, becomes your playbook. You update it without needing reminders, so she doesn't have to carry every detail in her head. Maybe you make it a habit to check that list every morning; if you see "call pediatrician" or "order more burp cloths," you just do it. These things don't go unnoticed; they add up

What matters most isn't perfection; it's effort that says "I'm here," "I care," and "We're doing this together." The little actions, the ones that might seem invisible, are often the ones that stick for years to come. Take pride in noticing what needs to be done without being told and acting before exhaustion sets in. That kind of support shifts everything, not just for your partner, but for your whole family.

Communication Scripts for Tough Conversations

Nobody tells you how awkward it can get trying to talk about the tough stuff when you're both running on caffeine, nerves, and barely three hours of sleep. You want to keep things calm, but sometimes it feels like any topic, who does more diapers, why nobody's in the mood for sex, or even who forgot to buy wipes, can turn into a standoff. Most couples hit this wall, and it's not a sign you're failing; it's just real life with a new baby.

What helps is having a few ready-to-go scripts for opening hard conversations without starting a fight. Start simple and keep your tone curious, not accusatory. Try: "I've noticed you seem distant lately. Can we talk about it?" or "I feel like we're both on edge. Is there something I'm missing?" For resentment, use gentle honesty: "It feels like I'm dropping the ball lately. How are you holding up?"

If the intimacy topic feels radioactive, approach it with vulnerability: "I miss being close. Can we figure out how to reconnect, even if it's just in small ways right now?" And for disagreements about parenting style, such as routine versus flexibility, screen time, or sleep training, open with, "I see things a little differently. Can we talk through what matters most to us?"

Active listening isn't rocket science, but it does take effort, especially when your brain is scattered and you're itching to jump in with a fix. The key is slowing down and echoing back what you hear: "What I'm hearing is that you feel overwhelmed and need help with bath time," or "So you're saying it stings when I correct you in front of your parents."

Use your body language to show you're present: put your phone down, make eye contact, nod occasionally, and resist the urge to cross your arms or roll your eyes. If you feel yourself clenching your jaw or staring out the window, reset by leaning forward a bit or mirroring your partner's posture. Sometimes physical cues speak louder than words.

When things start getting heated, it's easy to slip into fight-or-flight mode, voices rise, sarcasm creeps in, or someone storms off. Rather than letting arguments spiral, agree ahead of time on a "pause" word or gesture, a neutral phrase like "timeout," or even something silly like "banana," that signals you both need a break before saying something regrettable. If either of you calls for a pause, honor it without rolling your eyes or muttering under your breath. Step away for five minutes, splash cold water on your face, and come back when you're both less likely to escalate.

Checking in before tempers flare can save hours of silent treatment later. Schedule a weekly "relationship huddle." It sounds cheesy, but it works wonders. Choose a low-stress time (maybe after baby goes down for the night), grab snacks or tea, and ask each other three questions: *What went well this week? What was tough? How can I support you better next week?*

Use this space to hash out recurring issues, who gets up for the 4 a.m. feed, or how to handle grandparent visits, before resentment festers. My partner and I called this our "State of the Union," and some weeks we only lasted ten minutes before passing out, but even that short check-in kept us from bottling up annoyances.

Journaling before a hard talk helps clarify what's really bugging you. Jot down what you want to say and why it matters. Sometimes, writing out your thoughts cools the emotional charge before you open your mouth. Try prompts like: *What's really bothering me? What do I hope will change? Is there something I haven't said out loud yet?* You might realize you're not actually mad about dishes but feeling invisible after a rough week.

If you reach an impasse, say, nobody wants to be "the default parent" at night, try brainstorming together for creative fixes instead of sticking to old patterns. Maybe you alternate nights on duty, or use a coin toss for those extra-tough mornings. One dad shared how he and his wife used a shared calendar to plot out who handled which nights; another couple traded off early mornings versus late bedtimes based on work schedules.

The point isn't always perfect harmony. Sometimes, just knowing you can talk honestly without someone blowing up is enough. These scripts and routines turn conflict into connection, or at least keep things from boiling over. Real communication gets messy sometimes, but with practice and patience, it gets easier, and might even bring a few laughs at how hard both of you are trying.

Nighttime Feedings: How to Truly Share the Load

The reality of parenthood hits hardest during middle-of-the-night feedings. At 2 a.m., "sharing the load" isn't just a nice phrase; it's crucial to survival and sanity. When you wake up to a crying baby and lock eyes with your equally exhausted partner, know that this is the essence of early family life. There's no universal fix, but there are ways to make nights less stressful, more balanced, and a little less isolating.

Start by tailoring your approach to your family's feeding style. With bottle-fed babies, equality is possible: alternate nights or split the night into shifts (e.g., 7 p.m.–1 a.m. and 1 a.m.–7 a.m.), giving both parents a solid stretch of sleep. For breastfeeding families, teamwork has a different look. While only one parent can nurse, preparing bottles, water, and snacks before bed helps. Keep clean bottles and parts within arm's reach, prep a water bottle and snacks, and set up everything you'll need nearby. Partners can handle diaper changes and burping, allowing the nursing parent to focus only on feeding, then helping soothe the baby back to sleep.

Small gestures matter, especially if your partner is breastfeeding. Those moments when you might want to drift back to sleep, instead offer company, a back rub, water, or a quick snack. Even just sitting together can be a comfort and a reminder that you're in this together.

Fatigue often leads to resentment if left unchecked. The old "sleep when the baby sleeps" advice applies to both parents. Take turns napping and be fair with sleeping in after tough nights. Some couples set clear policies: if you're up for the first shift, go to bed after dinner while your partner handles bedtime routines, then switch for the next night or shift. Try trading mornings, too: one gets up early with the baby, the other sleeps in.

A bit of creativity goes a long way. Some couples keep a whiteboard in the kitchen to track shifts. A visual log helps clear up confusion and keeps things light in the haze of sleep deprivation. Others listen to audiobooks or podcasts during feeds, turning those early hours into a mini date. Sharing your "night shift playlist" or chatting about a book in the morning gives you something to look forward to and share.

Families with older kids might create visual schedules or magnet boards so everyone knows who's on duty, no confusion, no excuses. Working parents sometimes prep bottles before their shift, so their partner can grab and go with minimum fuss.

With combo feeding, you have more flexibility. Pumped milk or formula opens up the option for one parent to handle full overnight feeds while the other rests. Decide on a plan, alternate full nights off, or take turns every other night. Using formula or pumped milk so everyone gets rest is perfectly valid if it protects your family's well-being.

Small tweaks can make a big difference. Keeping a cooler with prepped bottles by your bed, or a stash of diapers, wipes, and pacifiers within reach, reduces nighttime scrambling. These adjustments can turn a chaotic night into a manageable one.

The emotional component shouldn't be overlooked. Sharing a joke, a glance, or a silly ritual can transform exhausting feeds into moments of connection. Some couples enjoy a nightly playlist or a goodnight phrase to bring routine and some lightness to sleep-deprived nights.

Open communication is key. If one partner feels overwhelmed or stuck with more than their share, talk about it and adjust your strategy together. Needs shift as babies grow, so stay flexible and regularly check in with each other to keep things fair.

Ultimately, no one gets enough sleep during these early months, but sharing night feeds is about more than rest; it's about ongoing commitment to each other. And sometimes, it's about finding a way to laugh together at 4 a.m., listening to an audiobook about Viking history, rocking your baby back to sleep, knowing you're not alone.

Navigating Physical Recovery: What Dads Need to Know

Watching your partner recover after childbirth is often a surprising challenge for new dads. Birth is hard on the body, whether it's a vaginal delivery, C-section, or a complicated experience. Recovery varies for everyone, but there are some constants.

Bleeding after birth is normal; think of a heavy period lasting a few weeks, meaning pads everywhere and absolutely no tampons. Pain is common too, sometimes sharp or just a dull ache. Vaginal births may involve swelling, stitches, or tearing, making sitting and moving uncomfortable. C-sections bring their own challenges: a surgical wound, strict lifting limits, and infection risk. Recovery timelines are personal. Some moms are up in a few days, others need weeks, but most take at least six weeks (sometimes more) to start feeling normal.

Mobility is usually difficult at first. Just getting out of bed or walking a short distance can hurt. For C-sections, your partner shouldn't lift anything heavier than the baby; the incision needs time to heal. That means you handle laundry baskets, older kids, the vacuum, and heavy lifting.

Watch for infection warning signs: redness, swelling, oozing, or fever, and call the doctor if you notice any. After a vaginal birth, keep an eye out for clots larger than a golf ball, foul-smelling discharge, or escalating pain. Any of these are reasons to call her OB or midwife.

Your main role right now is comfort. Help with whatever makes life easier. If standing or reaching hurts her, fetch the baby, carry the car seat, and push the stroller. Take care of pets or older kids so she can rest. Encourage her to sit and rest; you might need to insist. Jump in on practical tasks and let her know it's okay to take it easy.

What to avoid? Don't push her to "bounce back." Recovery is not a competition. Never question how long she's sore or suggest she should just "walk it off." Instead, set up comfortable spots for her to nurse or cuddle the baby, offer help with showers or dressing if needed, but back off if she wants space.

You can make a big difference through tangible tasks: Take over laundry, babies make a mountain of dirty clothes. Handle the washing, folding, and putting away so she doesn't have to ask. Take over kitchen duty: cook, clean, order in, and keep snacks handy. Take care of as many diaper changes as you can; it's more help than you'd think, sparing her extra bending and lifting. Keep the house tidy; even simple cleaning makes the home feel less chaotic, giving her one less thing to worry about.

Being an advocate is key. Relatives and friends may want to visit before your partner is ready. Be her gatekeeper: handle calls and texts, firmly say visits can wait, and don't let anyone pressure her to play host. At postpartum checkups, bring up questions: How's her bleeding? Is healing on track?

What's normal pain? Anything to watch for? Speak up if you need more info. Appointments can be rushed, and it's easy for concerns to get overlooked.

After my partner's C-section, I quickly realized how much more support she needed. She couldn't twist at all for the first week, so I handled diaper changes, stairs, and night rocking. We made a recovery nest in the living room so she could rest without moving much. I also learned how essential it was to set boundaries with family. Sometimes the best thing you can do is insist she rest, not entertain.

Recovery is often unpredictable, with good days and setbacks. But showing up, asking questions, running interference with visitors, and managing household duties gives your partner the space she needs to heal. That builds trust and shows you're truly in it together for every up and down ahead.

Team No Sleep: Surviving Together and Avoiding Resentment

Sleep deprivation is like a fog that settles in every corner of your house. It doesn't just steal your energy, it plays tricks on your mind, colors your mood, and tests your relationship in ways you never saw coming. You find yourself reaching for patience that just isn't there. Suddenly, small annoyances feel huge. You'll wonder why you're snapping at the person you love or why you both keep forgetting what you walked into the kitchen for.

Mood swings become routine, and frustration can rise out of nowhere. You may catch yourself feeling on edge, irritable, even a bit resentful about whose turn it is to change a diaper or who last woke up with the baby. This isn't a sign that something is wrong with you or your relationship; it's a completely normal response to chronic exhaustion. Your brain and body are simply stretched to their limit.

When everything feels overwhelming, survival mode kicks in. Instead of trying to do it all, it's time to divide and conquer. Honestly, this is the secret sauce for making it through those early months as a team. Sit down together and figure out who does what, even if you need to renegotiate every day. If one of you handles the morning shift, the other gets the next nap window, even if it's only twenty minutes stolen behind a closed door.

Scheduling mini-breaks isn't selfish; it's how you keep each other going. Maybe you agree that when one parent taps out, the other steps in without rolling their eyes or keeping score. A shared running joke can help. A silly code word for when exhaustion hits max level lets you both signal, "Hey, I'm about to lose it," without sparking a fight. My partner and I used "zombie mode" as our cue; one mention and we knew it was time for backup or a five-minute solo break. These tiny agreements build trust and buffer against resentment.

No matter how much you love each other, tired brains lead to sharp words. You might get snappy about nothing or bicker over whose turn it is to clean bottles, only to regret it an hour later. Learning how to apologize quickly is a huge relief for both of you. It's as simple as saying, "Sorry for snapping at you, I'm just exhausted." The key is not making excuses or dragging out the moment. Accept that tired arguments happen and let forgiveness flow faster than blame. Resetting after a rough patch means letting things go, don't rehash every squabble or keep a mental tally of mistakes. Sometimes, a quick hug or a shared laugh after an argument is all it takes to get back on the same side.

Small wins deserve big celebrations, especially on the nights when everything feels like chaos. Maybe your baby finally slept for three hours straight, or one of you managed to make coffee without waking the whole house. These victories may seem trivial from the outside, but inside your home, they're worth gold. One night, my partner and I hit our breaking point and just started dancing in the living room at 3 a.m., baby in arms, music on low, laughing so we wouldn't cry. That moment stuck with us as a reminder that sometimes silliness is survival.

Keeping a sense of humor helps soften the hardest nights. Share those "parent wins" out loud: "We both survived until sunrise!" or "Nobody cried during bath time!" If words aren't your thing, try jotting down small wins on sticky notes and plastering them somewhere visible: a fridge, bathroom mirror, or even the coffee maker. Over time, those colorful scraps become a wall of proof that you've weathered storms together and found joy in the mess.

A shared gratitude journal can work wonders too. Each night, write down one thing, no matter how small, that went right or made you smile. Maybe it's as simple as, "Thankful for five minutes of quiet," or "Loved your pancakes this morning." This tiny ritual shifts your focus from what's going wrong to what you're building together.

In the end, team no sleep isn't about thriving; it's about sticking together when things are tough and refusing to let exhaustion pull you apart. You'll look back on these nights someday with more pride than regret, not because they were easy, but because you got through them side by side.

Sleep deprivation will challenge your patience, humor, and bond with your partner, but facing it as a team makes all the difference. Stay united through exhaustion and arguments by leaning on each other and celebrating every win, no matter how small. Up next: we'll talk about balancing life outside the home, work, finances, and finding time for yourself, because keeping your family strong means taking care of every part of your life.

CHAPTER 5

Dad Health: Mental, Emotional, and Physical Well-being

Dad Stress Is Real: Recognizing the Signs

Picture yourself pacing the hallway at 4 a.m., cradling a fussy baby while your coffee sits untouched. You're exhausted, unsure if you're asleep or awake, and the pressure to be the steadfast dad can feel overwhelming. This is the unfiltered side of fatherhood few discuss, the kind of stress that's more than just lost sleep. Most new dads expect to be tired, but stress appears in far more forms than most realize.

It's one thing to feel tired; it's another to be so drained you forget what day it is. New dad stress often outlasts a good nap. You might feel a heavy weight that doesn't lift even after rest, or find yourself more irritable, snapping at small annoyances, like toys clattering or persistent phone alerts. Sometimes, you might instead feel numb and disconnected, almost like you're watching life happen from underwater. This isn't weakness; it's your mind dealing with overwhelm.

Physical symptoms of stress can be subtle. Maybe you're nursing daily headaches, digestive issues, tight shoulders, stubborn heartburn, or persistent muscle tension. If you find yourself reaching for painkillers or massaging your temples more than usual, your body is signaling that things aren't right.

Stress often builds slowly and subtly. You might pull away without noticing, spending time scrolling on your phone in another room rather than interacting with your partner or baby. Escapist habits like binge-watching, late-night snacking, or gaming can creep in, not from hunger or interest, but to avoid what's weighing on you. Trouble focusing is another sign: maybe you reread emails or forget simple tasks. If you find yourself zoning out or feeling like nothing "sticks," pay attention; these are classic stress signals.

What makes this tricky is that withdrawing or seeking distractions can seem harmless. Everyone needs downtime, but when withdrawal or constant tech use becomes your norm, it's a warning sign. Some dads mistake this for a "normal adjustment," but avoiding connection is different than recharging with some alone time.

It's hard to discern when everyday stress tips into something deeper, like depression, anxiety, or burnout. The line gets crossed when, for more than two weeks, you've lost interest in things you love, feel overwhelmed daily, or every day feels too much to handle. That's more than stress. Anxiety may hit as constant worry or restless energy, while burnout feels like unshakable exhaustion, no matter how much you sleep.

When to Worry: Quick Self-Check

- You feel hopeless or empty most days.
- You lose interest in old hobbies or what brings you joy.
- Sleep issues go beyond interrupted nights, insomnia, or wanting to sleep all the time.
- Small problems cause you to feel overwhelmed fast.
- It's tough to connect with your partner or baby for several days.

- Your appetite changes a lot (eating much more or less).
- You fantasize about escaping, not just for a short break, but disappearing.

If several of these signs are familiar and don't improve with time or simple support, consider reaching out for help.

You don't have to face this alone. Self-reflection isn't about blaming yourself; it's about noticing changes before they spiral. Try a weekly check-in with yourself: "What's different since the baby?" "Am I avoiding my family or favorite things?" "Is stress showing as anger or numbness?" If something feels off, that's important.

Many dads miss the signs: one dad took every night feed and extra work shift until his body gave out; another wrote off tension and mood swings as "normal tiredness," only to realize months later he hadn't really laughed in weeks. These aren't rare cases; they show that stress isn't always obvious.

Talking openly about stress matters. You wouldn't ignore your car's warning lights; don't ignore your own. Regularly checking in and being honest is the first step to feeling better and to being present for your family as your true self.

Five-Minute Reset: Micro Self-Care for Sleep-Deprived Dads

If you ever wondered who invented the phrase "running on fumes," it was probably a new dad. Between night feedings, endless laundry, and the day job that expects you to pretend you slept, your mind and body get stretched thin. The idea of "self-care" might make you roll your eyes. Who has time for bubble baths or long gym sessions? The good news is, you don't need hours or a Zen retreat to feel better. Micro self-care is about squeezing tiny, meaningful resets into the cracks of your day; five minutes here and there can have a bigger impact than you'd expect.

One of my go-to moves is box breathing. It's dead simple: breathe in for four seconds, hold for four, out for four, hold again for four. Repeat a few times. Try it in the car before walking back into the house, or while waiting for the bottle to warm up. If that feels too structured, the "4-7-8 method" is another option: inhale for four seconds, hold for seven, exhale for eight. This longer exhale helps your heart rate slow and signals your body to chill out, even when your brain's buzzing with a dozen worries at once. You don't need a mat, candles, or an app, just air and attention.

When you feel trapped indoors and your legs haven't moved except between the couch and the crib, step outside for a five-minute walk. Even just circling the block resets your headspace. Fresh air clears cobwebs and changes your perspective. If you can't leave the house, stretch it out: reach up, touch your toes, roll your shoulders. It's less about flexibility and more about breaking the "couch potato" spell that creeps in after hours of sitting or pacing with a baby in your arms.

For those times when escape seems impossible, even the bathroom can be your sanctuary. I call it "bathroom break meditation." Lock the door, close your eyes, and just notice the feeling of sitting still. Nobody's asking you for anything. You get one minute just to hear yourself breathe. Don't feel guilty, everyone needs a moment to hit pause, even if it's behind a closed door.

Music changes everything. Pop in headphones for a favorite song; even half a song can jolt your mood out of a spiral. Or fire up a short podcast segment; five minutes of laughter or a voice you enjoy helps you reset. If you're feeding the baby solo, let a playlist run in the background while you rock.

Suddenly, even the most repetitive routine feels less isolating.

Some days, creativity is required to snag rest. Power naps in the car, those 10 minutes reclined in the driveway, sometimes feel like winning the lottery. If naps aren't possible, try a two-minute gratitude journal in your notes app or on a sticky note. Write three things that didn't suck today: "baby smiled at me," "coffee was hot," "partner laughed at my joke." Small moments matter more than big ones when you're running low.

You don't need elaborate prep or fancy equipment for these resets. Dad hacks are all about making use of what's at hand. Stash a snack in the glove box for late-night drives back from the store. Keep a reusable water bottle nearby. You'll be shocked at how often dehydration feels like exhaustion or crankiness. If your partner is around, tag them in and step outside for a deep breath or two under the sky.

These micro-breaks aren't selfish; they're fuel for better parenting. Taking five minutes for yourself can flip your mood from "I can't deal" to "I've got this." You'll catch yourself snapping less, listening with more patience, and actually enjoying the little moments rather than wishing them away. I remember one meltdown evening where I almost lost my temper over spilled milk (literally). I put my son down safely in his crib, stepped outside for five long breaths, and came back with enough calm to clean up and laugh about it later.

Mood Shift Visual: Before and After Micro-Break

Draw a quick chart in your journal with two columns: "Before Break" and "After Break." Rate your mood from 1 (frazzled) to 10 (chill). Notice how even a five-minute reset can bump you up a notch or two on that scale.

Don't underestimate these tiny routines. When used regularly, they stack up to real change: your patience grows, frustration fades faster, and you recover from setbacks with more ease. It's not about being perfect; it's about giving yourself permission to pause before you reach your breaking point. Small resets teach your brain, and your family, that dads deserve care too.

When to Ask for Help: A No-Shame FAQ

Admitting you're struggling, especially as a new dad, can be tough. There's an old myth that you should handle everything alone, tough it out, and never let anyone see you struggle. Maybe you've told yourself, "Just man up," or "It's just tiredness." But thinking like that keeps many dads from getting the help they need. Pride, fear of judgment, or not wanting to look weak builds walls between you and support that could make things better. Many dads wait months before reaching out, thinking asking for help means failure, but it actually means you care enough to want things to improve.

Wondering if your feelings are "normal" is common. Everyone feels off sometimes, but if you're stuck, constant irritability, sadness, or feeling disconnected from your family, it's worth talking about. Maybe you aren't sleeping, you're snapping at everyone, or you keep thinking your family would be better off without you. If these feelings last more than a couple of weeks, don't ignore them. Reaching out sooner can help things get better faster.

Starting the conversation doesn't have to be complicated. If talking to your partner feels awkward, try saying: "I haven't been feeling like myself," or "I think I need to talk to someone, even if I'm not sure what's wrong." You don't need to have it all figured out, just open the door. With friends, honesty is key. Say, "Hey, have you ever felt like you can't get out of a funk?" or "I could use some backup right now." You might find they've felt the same and are ready to listen. If you'd rather not talk face-to-face, a text or a meme can also help break the ice.

Talking to a doctor might seem intimidating, but you won't be the first new parent they've seen. Simply say, "I'm having trouble coping since the baby arrived. I feel anxious, sad, or angry all the time." They'll guide you from there and suggest resources that suit you. If you're concerned you'll forget details, jot down a few notes before your appointment: main symptoms, when they started, and what makes them better or worse.

Here's a quick FAQ for dads:

- **"Is it normal to feel this bad?"**
  Short-term stress is expected; if misery or hopelessness lingers, it's time to reach out.

- **"Will people think less of me if I ask for help?"**
  No. Most people respect honesty and courage.

Asking for help is about caring for your family, not your ego.

- **"What if I don't know what to say?"**
Start with "I'm not okay," or "I need some support." That's enough.

- **"Who do I call?"**
If things are urgent, like thoughts of self-harm, call a helpline right away. For ongoing stress, reach out to your doctor or a therapist.

Quick Resource List for Dads Ready to Reach Out

- **National hotlines:** Call the National Suicide Prevention Lifeline (1-800-273-8255) 24/7.
- **Dad-specific support:** Postpartum Support International offers a dad helpline and online chat.
- **Apps:** Try Headspace for mindfulness or Moodfit for mood tracking.
- **Local groups:** Search Facebook or Meetup for local or virtual new dad groups.
- **Therapists:** Use Psychology Today to find local therapists, including those specializing in men's and fathers' mental health.

Other dads confirm: asking for help changes things. One dad wrote, "The first call was the hardest, but all I got was understanding." Another said, "My partner just wanted honesty. When I opened up, we both cried, but we started solving things together."

A favorite quote from a dad: "I thought real strength was never needing help. Turns out, real strength is asking for it anyway." There's no reward for suffering in silence.

Sometimes the bravest thing is admitting you're not okay and taking the first step toward feeling better. Your family needs you healthy and happy, not just toughing it out every day.

Managing Anxiety About "Doing It Right"

If you've ever sat holding your squirming baby, heart pounding with worries of "Am I messing this up?" you're not alone. Nearly every dad feels some level of anxiety about being "good enough." Nobody warns you that self-doubt comes standard with parenthood. There's constant pressure to get it all right: bottle temps, sleep schedules, diaper changes, partner support, and work responsibilities. It feels like spinning plates half-asleep, with more plates added for good measure. But perfection isn't the goal. You just need to keep showing up and trying.

Those sudden thoughts, "What if I drop her?" or "I'm the worst at this," are way more common than you might think. They don't mean you're falling apart; they mean your brain is handling something new. Often, our minds fixate on worst-case scenarios not because they'll happen, but because you care deeply. Self-doubt isn't a failure; it's proof you're engaged and trying. The trick is not letting these worries control you.

Start managing anxious moments by noticing them as they arise. If your mind is looping a mistake or dread for the next meltdown, try grounding yourself. Practice naming five things you see, four you can touch, three you hear, two you smell, and one you taste. Anchor yourself in the present; it's usually less scary than what's in your head.

Another tool: box breathing. Inhale for four counts, hold for four, exhale for four, hold for four more. Repeat until you feel yourself relax. This calms your nervous system and signals that panic isn't needed.

Consider jotting down a "parent win" at the end of the day, even something small, like remembering an extra onesie or smiling through a rough patch. These victories often vanish in the fog of anxiety, but collecting them shows you're more capable than your inner critic says.

Mistakes will happen, sometimes funny, sometimes awkward, but if you treat them as lessons rather than proof you're failing, they're valuable. The first time I forgot the diaper bag, I dried my kid off with my shirt in a Target bathroom. Embarrassing, sure, but I learned to double-check before leaving the house and keep a spare in the car. Reflect on these moments with, "What did I learn?" instead of, "Why do I suck?" One dad shared he once snapped a onesie over pajamas and only noticed at bedtime. Everyone laughed, and no harm was done.

Expectations can trip you up. Comparing yourself to Instagram dads or impossible standards will only feed anxiety. Instead, write your own "dad job description," what's important to you, not what others expect. Maybe it's "Be present at bedtime" or "Stay patient when things are loud." Your list should be uniquely yours. Great dads aren't perfect; they're real, adaptable, and willing to apologize and restart.

Grab a notebook or your phone and, in a few lines, jot down what matters most to you as a parent, not what your parents did or what social media dictates. Maybe it's raising a kind child or bringing laughter to tough days. Use these as your guiding principles when anxiety sneaks in.

Nobody becomes Superdad overnight, and anyone who says otherwise is exaggerating or forgetting. Your child doesn't need perfect; they need present, honest, and loving. Showing up, even when you mess up, builds trust and resilience in both of you. Allow yourself to be imperfect, laugh off your mistakes, and keep going, even on the worst days.

Anxiety grows in silence. Sharing your worries with another dad or even writing them down reduces their power. Some days will feel chaotic; others will be quieter but heavy with self-doubt. That's part of parenting, not a sign you're not enough.

A year from now, your child won't remember if you folded a swaddle perfectly or did voices in stories just right. What they'll remember is that you were there, imperfect, genuine, loving, which is exactly what "doing it right" looks like.

Building Your Dad Support Squad (Without Forced Small Talk)

I never pictured myself searching for "dad friends," but parenthood has a way of changing social habits. Early on, I thought I could handle everything on my own, but isolation gradually crept in. Most new dads don't imagine themselves joining dad groups or swapping diaper tips in crowded cafes; forced small talk or awkward meetups just feel exhausting, especially if you're an introvert or tired of talking about the weather. Still, finding your people, even in unlikely places, can really lighten those long, draining days.

Support often shows up where you least expect it. Sometimes it's at work, like noticing a tired coworker with spit-up on his shirt and sharing a knowing look. A simple "Rough night?" or a quick chat by the coffee machine can spark a genuine connection without any pressure. Hobbies are another goldmine: fantasy football leagues, BBQ groups, or video game sessions tend to drift from stats to stories about parenting chaos. Online spaces like Reddit's r/daddit or local Facebook groups fill a gap, making it easy to share struggles and advice without face-to-face pressure.

Reaching out doesn't mean baring your soul in a group circle. Low-effort connections work well. Text threads, for instance, let dads swap memes about sleepless nights or share photos of parenting disasters. Humor helps break the ice and reminds you you're not alone. Prefer something a bit more active? Organize a dad-and-baby coffee walk, no deep talks, just caffeine, strollers, and the option to chat as you wander. These low-key hangouts are perfect if you dislike structure but want connection.

If you're nervous about reaching out, start small. You don't have to share your deepest struggles, send a funny meme about new dad life, or drop an article link in a group chat. It's often easier to connect over humor or shared stories than to launch into heavy topics. Gradually, these little check-ins become anchors: a simple "How's everyone's sleep?" or "Anyone else dealing with teething?" often leads to honest, judgment-free replies.

Maintaining these connections doesn't take a lot of effort, even when you're busy. Group chats are a lifesaver: they let you reply on your own time. Set up regular check-ins, maybe Sunday nights, everyone shares a "dad win" from the week, big or small (like surviving a blowout or getting a smile after a rough morning). These small rituals create camaraderie and keep everyone engaged without taking up much time.

Your support squad doesn't need to be big; just two or three dads you trust can make a difference. Swapping tips about bottles or venting about tantrums creates real bonds, sometimes deeper than pre-parent friendships. You'll get advice you didn't know you needed, like how to remove spit-up stains or which parks have the best playgrounds. Helping another dad through a tough moment also boosts your own mood. Perspective doubles when shared.

One night, after my daughter screamed for hours, I sent a panicked message to my group chat: "Is this normal, or do I have a banshee?" Instantly, two dads chimed in with solidarity. One even sent a meme that made me laugh and snap out of my spiral. At the playground, a simple conversation about diaper bags became a regular Saturday meet-up and a lasting friendship. Moments like these don't require emotional speeches or planned events; just showing up however you can is enough.

Your support system might look different; maybe it's your brother, a college friend with twins, or a neighbor you pass on stroller walks. The essential part is openness: share a bit of your real, messy day. Don't wait for someone else to start the conversation; sometimes one honest text or a coffee walk is all it takes to shift from struggling alone to thriving together.

There's no manual for fatherhood, but strength multiplies in numbers, even if it's just two guys swapping memes at midnight while their babies wail. Connection doesn't need scripts or ceremonies; it just needs honesty, willingness to reach out, and maybe even the occasional emoji.

Embracing the Dad Bod: Health, Wellness, and Self-Compassion

The "dad bod," a term often joked about in memes and casual banter, carries pressures of both pride and shame. While the soft edges might spark humor, they're also evidence of late nights, skipped workouts, and meals eaten on the go while juggling parenting. Right now, forget pursuing a six-pack; your real achievement is simply being present for your family in whatever shape you're in.

Redefining fitness as a new dad means dropping the pursuit of perfection. Instead, focus on movement that fits your current life: squats while holding your baby, couch push-ups, hallway lunges during nap time, or stroller "runs" that are sometimes more determined walks. The goal isn't beating old gym records; it's about feeling good and having the energy to keep up with your little one. Leave behind old standards; this is a new chapter with new priorities.

When it comes to eating, the kitchen doesn't have to be a source of stress. Keep it simple: prep snacks like granola bars, cut fruit, and yogurt in batches to avoid less healthy options. Rely on one-pot dinners and slow cooker meals to save time. Planning lunches (even leftovers) prevents slipping into fast food habits that leave you sluggish. If you didn't prep meals before your baby arrived, lean on pre-washed greens, rotisserie chicken, and ready-made grains. Eating well isn't about strict "clean eating," it's about fueling yourself so you can keep going.

Sleep is a major challenge for new dads. Advice to "sleep when the baby sleeps" often feels unhelpful, but every minute counts. Share night shifts with your partner if you can; short naps can be surprisingly restorative. If you're alone, try to nap near your baby or during an afternoon feed. Use a sleep mask for daytime naps, and don't feel guilty for prioritizing rest over chores; no one can function on no sleep for long.

Physical self-care connects directly with your mood and patience. A quick walk after a rough morning can reset your mind. A good meal does more than stop hunger; it can elevate your mood and help with irritability. Your body may have changed, but it's working hard for you each day, and that's worth respecting.

Practicing gratitude towards your body means focusing on what it accomplishes now, not what it did in the past. Maybe you lugged a stroller up the stairs, rocked your baby to sleep for hours, or simply endured another hectic day. These actions display strength. The first time pushing a stroller while running might feel awkward, but those shared moments are what matter, not your speed or style.

Looking in the mirror and appreciating your body's stretch marks, scars, or softness takes courage. These marks record your efforts and care. Instead of chasing a perfect ideal, ask yourself: "What did my body do for me today?" Did you comfort your baby, carry groceries and the car seat, or dance through a tough evening? These small victories mean more than any unattainable standard.

A helpful reflection exercise is to jot down one thing your body accomplished today, even if it was just making it through another sleep-deprived day. These notes become reminders that health is about energy, presence, and resilience, not just appearances.

Ultimately, the "dad bod" is a badge of involvement, showing that your priorities have shifted for the better. You're exchanging gym time for precious moments on the playmat or with bottles at 2 a.m. It might not feel glamorous, but it's true strength.

Physical health as a new dad isn't about achieving perfection. It's about small, sustainable choices, a little grace, and gratitude for what your body achieves day by day. The dad bod isn't a punchline, it's earned, one sleepless night at a time.

Next, we'll talk about tracking your baby's milestones and knowing when to worry, so you can focus your energy where it matters most.

CHAPTER 6

Navigating Milestones and Emergencies: What's Normal, What's Not

Customizable Dad-Friendly Milestone Trackers

The first time I saw my baby grin, it hit me like a lightning bolt, just a gummy, crooked smile that made every sleepless night worth it. I didn't need a book to know it was special, but I did wonder, "Is this early? Late? Should I write this down?" Enter milestone trackers. Not the overwhelming kind, but simple tools you can actually use without guilt if you miss a few boxes or dates. Your baby doesn't care about perfect checklists; they care about you cheering them on.

Let's break milestones down by month, but remember: "normal" covers a wide range. Some babies roll over at three months, others at five. Some babble at six months, others wait until nine to say their first "da-da." The CDC and other sources highlight these windows for good reason: babies aren't robots on the same timeline. Key first-year milestones generally include: first real smile (6–8 weeks), holding eye contact (by 2 months), rolling from tummy to back (around 4 months), big laughs or babbling (4–6 months), sitting up with support (6 months), crawling/scooting (8–10 months), standing with help, and those first wobbly steps by one year. Every milestone has an early, average, and late window. Some babies skip crawling and jump straight to walking, while others focus on fine motor skills before saying "mama."

Every month, jot down what stands out, even if it isn't in a baby book. Maybe your highlight is that first moment of eye contact or a funny little wiggle you won't find on any milestone chart. You decide what's important. I encourage you to create your own tracker. A one-page sheet on your fridge or a note in your phone is perfect. Enter the classic markers for each month: smile (6–8 weeks), eye contact (2 months), rolling (4 months), laughing (4–5 months), babbling (6 months), sitting (6–7 months), crawling (8–10 months), pulling to stand (9–12 months), first steps (anytime between 9–18 months). Next to each, leave a "Dad Win" space for your own memorable moments, even if it's just

"Slept through (sort of)," or "Made her giggle with my goofy dance moves."

If it feels like your baby is behind, don't panic. Every milestone has its own range, and being late doesn't always mean something is wrong. If your baby isn't rolling at five months but seems alert, that's often fine. If they sit up at nine months instead of six but are progressing in other areas, that's likely still normal. Delays are only worrisome with other red flags: sudden loss of skills, extreme stiffness/floppiness, no social smiles or eye contact by four months, or total silence and no gestures by ten months. In such cases, contact your pediatrician and trust your instincts; you know your child best. Otherwise, relax and focus on steady progress instead of dates.

Comparison is a trap. Social media makes it seem like every baby is sprinting ahead, but you rarely see the struggles and delays behind the scenes. Celebrate each little step with pride, whether it's a first giggle, stubborn crawl, or your own success at changing a diaper without disaster.

Dad Milestone Reflection Prompt

At the end of each month, spend a few minutes filling this in:

"Proud moment of the month:_____"

It can be any little win: a new skill, a silly face, or just surviving a tough week together.

Take a photo, jot a note on your phone, or share it with your partner. These moments add up quickly and tell the real story of your first year as a dad.

Remember, this year isn't about perfect timing; it's about being present for the big and small moments unique to your child's journey. Your baby needs you to show up and cheer them on, no matter their individual timeline.

Red Flags and Real Emergencies: Dad's Guide to Baby Health

Every parent eventually faces that moment of panic: a strange rash, an unsettling cough, or a high fever. Deciding whether to shrug it off, call the pediatrician, or rush to the

ER can feel overwhelming. A simple green, yellow, red system can help. Green means "don't panic," for minor sniffles, mild spit-up, or a harmless rash. Yellow means "be alert," for a low-grade fever, unusual fussiness, or odd-looking poop, but your baby is still mostly acting normal. Red means "take action now," for high fevers, especially in babies under three months, labored breathing with ribs pulling in, grunting, or flared nostrils, blue lips, ongoing vomiting, or seizures. Eating problems, like refusing two feeds in a row or having no wet diapers for eight hours, also warrant a call. Watch for sudden limpness, a bulging soft spot on the head, or a rash that doesn't blanch when pressed.

Emergencies can hit in the middle of the night and make you question everything. For babies under three months with a fever over 100.4°F/38°C, call your doctor immediately. For older babies, consider both the number and behavior. If they're hard to wake, extremely irritable, wheezing, or refusing fluids, seek help. Breathing issues are serious; if you see blue lips, retractions, grunting, or head bobbing, call 911 or go to the ER. Vomiting is usually manageable, but becomes urgent if it's projectile, recurring, or contains blood or green bile. Any seizure, shaking, or loss of consciousness requires immediate care.

Here are quick responses to common emergencies:

- **High fever**: Use a rectal thermometer, keep the baby lightly dressed, offer fluids, monitor for other symptoms (rash, stiff neck, odd cry). Call the doctor right away if under three months; call if there are additional red flag symptoms in older babies.
- **Breathing trouble**: Check for chest retractions, stridor (high-pitched wheeze), or if your baby is too breathless to feed. Keep your baby upright and call emergency services.
- **Non-stop vomiting**: Watch for dehydration: dry mouth, absent tears, no wet diapers. Offer small sips of oral rehydration solution; contact your pediatrician.
- **Seizures**: Lay your baby safely on their side, don't put anything in their mouth, time the episode if you can, and call 911.

Communicating clearly during emergencies helps healthcare providers respond quickly. Start with your baby's age and core symptoms: "I have a 2-month-old with a 101°F fever, who won't wake for feeds." Explain how long it's been happening, what you've tried, and all symptoms, e.g., "She has a red rash on her legs that doesn't fade when pressed." The more specific, the better.

Use a script: "Hi, I'm calling about my [baby's age]. [Symptom] started [when], now she's also [other symptoms]. [Number] wet diapers in [hours], and I'm worried because [reason]." Take notes on their instructions and repeat them back.

From my rookie parent days: One night, I saw purple spots on my daughter's legs and panicked, fearing the worst. At urgent care, the doctor calmly diagnosed a harmless newborn rash, and it disappeared by morning. Moral: It's okay to overreact when you're unsure, especially at first. Keeping a record of vitals (temperature, diaper counts) and focusing on breathing helped me stay calm until we saw a doctor.

Staying level-headed in emergencies is tough, but it is possible. Take three big breaths before acting. Focus on measurable facts: temperature, color, breathing patterns, and diapers. Ask for help. Healthcare providers would much rather reassure you than have you go it alone. Save emergency contacts in your phone, and jot down key details when things are calm so you're ready. Overreact once or twice? That just means you care and are ready for real emergencies when they come.

When Baby Won't Eat, Sleep, or Stop Crying: Troubleshooting

Picture this: it's the middle of the night, you're holding a red-faced, wailing baby and wondering how someone so small can produce that much noise. Whether it's feeding refusal, epic sleep struggles, or a meltdown that just won't quit, every dad hits this wall sooner or later. Instead of letting panic take the wheel, you can break these moments down with clear, step-by-step logic. Think of it as your "dad decision tree." This isn't about being perfect; it's about staying calm and figuring out what's actually going on, one step at a time.

Start with feeding refusal. If your baby turns away from the bottle or breast or outright refuses to eat, pause before going into fix-it mode. Sometimes, babies just aren't hungry yet. First, check for obvious issues: is your baby too sleepy? Try waking with a gentle diaper change or undressing down to the diaper for a bit of cool air. Next, inspect the feeding equipment. Sometimes the bottle nipple gets clogged or the milk temperature is off. If breastfeeding, see if a different position helps or if there's a latch problem (cracked nipples, dribbling milk, or clicking sounds are clues). If your baby is fussy but alert and peeing as usual, try again in 30 minutes. A stuffy nose can make sucking hard; use a bulb syringe or saline drops if needed. If your baby skips more than two feeds in a row or seems listless, call your pediatrician.

Now for sleep struggles: your baby's eyes are wide open at 2 a.m., or they doze off only to wake howling minutes later. First question, hungry? Try a feed, especially if it has been over two hours. Not hungry? Check the diaper. Still fussing? Is the room too hot or cold? Adjust layers and try again. Next, look for gas. Burp gently or cycle their legs like a slow-motion bicycle. White noise machines or apps (even just a running fan) can sometimes settle overstimulated babies. Avoid rocking all night or letting them nap in unsafe places (like car seats outside the car), even if it's tempting in exhaustion. Resist the urge to overfeed just to get more sleep; babies spit up more when overfull.

When crying is the main event and nothing soothes them, it's time to go step by step. Start with the basics: hunger, diaper, temperature. Move to burping and gentle movement (walks, rocking). Try changing scenery. Take your baby to a different room or stand by a window. Dimming the lights and lowering noise levels helps overstimulated little ones settle down. For some, a pacifier works wonders; for others, swaddling (if safe and the baby isn't rolling yet) can calm frazzled nerves. If all else fails, skin-to-skin time might help both of you relax.

Common mistakes crop up in these moments. It's easy to overfeed in hopes of silencing cries. Resist the urge unless you're sure hunger is the issue. Don't layer on extra sleep props like loose blankets or stuffed animals; they're unsafe for babies under one year old. Avoid panicking over normal newborn fussiness. Some babies simply cry more than others, especially in the evenings (a phase often called "the witching hour"). Myths like "letting them cry strengthens their lungs" are outdated. Babies need comfort and support, not tough love, at this age.

Knowing when to call for backup is key. If you've run your troubleshooting checklist, fed, changed, burped, checked temperature and environment, and your baby is still inconsolable after two hours or shows new symptoms (fever, vomiting, limpness, trouble breathing), it's time to reach out. Your partner should always be in the loop; sometimes just swapping shifts and getting fresh eyes on the situation makes all the difference. Don't hesitate to call your pediatrician if your gut says something's off. For crying specifically, most healthy newborns cry up to three hours a day (yes, really), but if it seems excessive or you're getting worried about dehydration (no wet diapers in 6–8 hours), medical advice is a good move.

The real secret is learning to trust yourself and this logical flow: Is my baby hungry? No? Wet? No? Gassy? Tried burping? Too hot/cold? Environment overstimulating? If you've checked every box and still feel lost, that's normal too; it happens to everyone at some point. Taking a break (putting baby safely in their crib and stepping away for five minutes) is not only okay, it's sometimes necessary for your own sanity. Remember, you're not alone on those tough nights; every dad has faced down a marathon cry session and come out on the other side with new skills (and maybe a few more gray hairs). The more you follow these steps, the easier it gets to spot what works for your unique kid, and your confidence will build right alongside theirs.

Sleep Regression Survival: Why It Happens and What to Do

There's a night when you're certain you've cracked the code. Your baby falls asleep early, stays down for a few glorious hours, and you start to believe the worst is over. Then, out of nowhere, your champion sleeper transforms into a pint-sized insomniac, waking every hour, wailing for reasons that seem to change by the minute. If you've hit this wall, you might be smack in the middle of a sleep regression. A phase when your baby's sleep takes a nosedive just as you were getting comfortable. Sleep regressions are notorious for showing up at predictable times: around four months, again at eight months, and another wave near the first birthday. They're not random; they tend to coincide with rapid brain growth, learning new tricks (like rolling or standing), or when separation anxiety kicks in and your baby suddenly needs to check that you haven't disappeared into an alternate dimension every 25 minutes.

Understanding why these regressions happen actually helps. During the four-month regression, your baby's sleep pattern matures and becomes more like an adult's, with lighter sleep cycles and frequent waking. At eight months, crawling,

129

pulling up, and growing curiosity mean brains are busy even at midnight. The twelve-month phase often overlaps with walking and a big burst in language, as babies want to practice their new skills at any hour. It's not bad parenting or something you did; it's biology and development doing their thing. This doesn't make it less exhausting, but at least you know there's a reason behind the chaos.

When you're in the thick of regression nights, routines become your anchor. Stick to a consistent bedtime routine: bath, pajamas, favorite book or song, dim lights. Babies thrive on repetition; the predictability signals that sleep is coming, even if they fight it.

If your baby wakes often, keep interactions boring and calm. No bright lights, no wild games, just soothing whispers and gentle pats. Swapping "night duty" with your partner can save your sanity; take turns or split the night into shifts so both of you get some rest. Tag-teaming isn't just practical; it keeps resentment from building up in the darkness.

Try comfort objects if your baby is old enough (a soft blanket or safe lovey), white noise for blocking out distracting sounds, and keep the crib clear of clutter. If your baby wants to practice standing or crawling in the crib, give them plenty of floor time during the day to burn off that energy.

Surviving these nights takes more than strategy; it takes grit and a willingness to let go of perfect expectations. You'll feel frustration boiling over sometimes. You'll question whether you're doing something wrong. It's normal to look in the mirror and think, *"How do people survive this?"*

The emotional punch of sleep deprivation is real: short tempers, blank stares, sometimes even tears at 3 a.m. Remind yourself: every dad has watched the clock crawl through the early hours and felt like he's failing. This doesn't mean you're weak; it means you care. Lower your standards for a while; if everyone is fed and safe, that's enough. Keep humor close by. Share "Team No Sleep" war stories with other dads. Text a friend who gets it or scroll through those tired dad memes on your phone at 4 a.m. Sometimes just knowing you're not alone makes those long nights feel less soul-crushing.

Of course, there are moments when sleep issues cross the line from normal regression into something that needs attention. Trust your gut if you see extreme lethargy, your baby can't stay awake for feeds or playtime, or if breathing seems labored or noisy beyond regular newborn sounds. If your child refuses all food and liquids for more than eight hours or has fewer than three wet diapers in 24 hours during these phases, call your doctor. Pay close attention to high fevers or any sign your baby is struggling to breathe comfortably while lying down. These aren't just bumps on the sleep regression road; they're signals that call for professional advice. Don't wait and wonder; reach out for help.

Sleep regressions can feel like a never-ending loop of "why won't you just sleep?" followed by coffee-fueled mornings where you wonder if you'll ever think straight again. The truth is, these phases eventually pass, even if it feels impossible in the moment. Every time you get through a rough night, you're building resilience, not just for your baby but for yourself too. You learn to adapt, improvise, and find small victories where you can, like celebrating a two-hour stretch of unbroken sleep as if you've won an award. This isn't about being superhuman; it's about hanging on, together, until the storm passes and a new stage begins.

Tummy Time and Development: Making It Work (Even with Protests)

Tummy time sounds simple, but if you're like most new dads, the first time you put your baby on their stomach, you get a lot of protest and a face that says, "Why are you doing this to me?"

Here's the thing: tummy time is way more than a baby workout. It's a daily boost for your kid's physical and brain growth. When your little one pushes up on their arms, even for a few seconds, they're building neck strength, shoulder stability, and the core muscles that set the stage for rolling, crawling, and eventually walking. Plus, spending time on their tummy helps prevent those flat spots on the back of the head that come from too much lying down. It also encourages visual tracking and hand coordination. Your baby learns to reach, bat at toys, and eventually scoot toward something interesting. Cognitive skills get a boost too, because every wobbly push-up is a lesson in cause and effect.

Doctors say you should aim for tummy time from day one, just a minute or two at first, working up to about an hour total by three months old. Don't worry; your baby doesn't have to do it all at once. You can break it up into lots of short sessions throughout the day. Think of it as practice, not a test. Your lap counts. Lying on your chest counts. Even propping your baby up over your arm while you watch TV together is fair game. The main thing is to make it a habit and keep adding a little more each week.

If you want to make it fun (or at least less terrible), try mixing things up. Babies love faces more than anything. Get down at their level and smile, make funny noises, or stick out your tongue. Try using mirrors; most babies are fascinated by their own reflection (and if you're honest, it's kind of hilarious seeing that confused stare). Bring in favorite toys or bright rattles and place them just out of reach to encourage reaching and swiping. Sometimes what works best is the old-school move: lean back on the couch with your shirt off and put your baby belly-down on your chest. That skin-to-skin time counts as tummy time and feels safe for both of you. And if your baby fusses after ten seconds, that's completely normal. Pick them up, give them a break, then try again later.

Of course, not every session goes smoothly. Some babies seem to hate tummy time with a passion. They'll cry, flip over, or just bury their face and refuse to move. This isn't a sign you're doing things wrong; some kids resist because it feels strange or hard at first. If your baby rolls right over or fusses nonstop, don't take it personally. You can try singing their favorite silly song or narrating what you see: "Whoa! You're so strong!" Sometimes joining them on the floor does the trick. Lie down right beside your baby so they feel like they have company in the struggle. Try moving them to different rooms or changing up the scenery with soft blankets or patterned mats.

Keep sessions short if needed; two to three minutes is fine to start. Gradually add a bit more time as your baby gets stronger and more comfortable. Celebrate every win: that first time they lift their head for longer than five seconds; the moment they prop up on elbows instead of face-planting; that hesitant kick that finally rolls them onto their back. Each bit of progress is worth cheering about.

Here's a dad hack that actually helps: keep a log or chart, nothing fancy; even tally marks on your fridge work. Write down how many minutes your baby spends each day on their tummy and what new moves you spot. Did they push up higher this week? Did they finally reach for that stuffed giraffe? Snap photos if you want; a quick before-and-after series can show how far you've both come in just a few weeks.

Some of my proudest moments as a dad happened during these sessions, not just because my kid got better at tummy time, but because I was there cheering him on, clapping like a fool when he finally found his balance. You'll have days when your baby screams through the whole thing and days when they surprise you with sudden strength or curiosity. It's all progress, even the messy, noisy parts count.

The key is to stay patient and flexible. If today's session is a disaster, try again later or switch up your approach. If you're consistent (and forgiving), your baby will grow stronger and more confident, and you'll rack up those "dad win" moments that make all the difference in these early months.

Vaccines, Checkups, and What to Actually Worry About

Staying on top of vaccines and checkups is one of those things that sounds simple on paper but always feels like a logistical puzzle in real life. The baby's first year is jam-packed with appointments, each with its own set of shots and questions. If you're like most new dads, you want to know what's coming up and how to make those doctor visits less of an ordeal for everyone involved. Let's break it down so you can show up ready, not scrambling.

The first-year vaccine schedule is pretty standard, and most pediatricians will hand you a printout, but it helps to have a dad-specific cheat sheet. At birth, your baby gets the first dose of Hepatitis B (usually right in the hospital). At two months, expect a flurry: DTaP (diphtheria, tetanus, pertussis), Polio, Hib (Haemophilus influenzae type b), PCV13 (pneumococcal), and Rotavirus. Four months brings repeat doses of all these except Hep B. Six months is similar, another round of DTaP, Polio, Hib, PCV13, Hep B, and Rotavirus. Around twelve months, it's time for MMR (measles, mumps, rubella), Varicella (chickenpox), Hepatitis A, and another PCV13 shot. If you're a checklist person, print this out or set reminders on your phone. Add the date and jot down any reactions or questions after each visit.

Knowing what's routine at each visit helps you relax before the appointment. Most checkups involve measuring weight and length, getting a head circumference, checking reflexes, and talking about feeding, sleep, and milestones. Your doctor will often ask about what your baby is doing: rolling over, grabbing toys, babbling, or making eye contact. Sometimes it feels like a pop quiz on your own kid. Don't stress if you can't remember every detail; bring notes or even videos if you want to highlight something new (or weird) you've noticed.

When it comes to vaccines, most babies will have some mild side effects, maybe a little fever (under 101°F), some crankiness, more sleepiness than usual, or swelling at the shot site. These are normal and usually clear up in a day or two. A cool washcloth or baby-safe pain reliever (if approved by your doc) can help. What's not normal is a persistent high fever (over 103°F), swelling that keeps getting worse or turns hard and red, trouble breathing, or extreme listlessness after shots. If you see any of these red flags, call your pediatrician right away.

Advocating for your kid at these appointments doesn't mean grilling your doctor on every detail, but don't hold back if something feels off or you're just confused. It's totally fine to say, "I'm worried about this rash," or "He doesn't make eye contact like other babies at daycare, is that okay?" Some good questions for your toolkit:

- "Is this delay in rolling, sitting, or whatever milestone—something I should worry about?"
- "How can I make recovery easier for my partner after delivery or surgery?"
- "Are there ways to make shots less stressful for my baby?"
- "If I notice [symptom], should I call right away or just watch it?"

If you forget what you meant to ask by the time the doctor walks in (it happens to all of us), keep a running note on your phone or use a sticky note in the diaper bag. Jot down anything weird or new during the week, odd poops, new habits, feeding quirks, so your mind doesn't go blank when the pediatrician looks at you.

Doctor visits are smoother with a little prep work. Pack a "doctor bag" before leaving: favorite small toy or pacifier (distraction is everything), feeding supplies (bottle or snack if age-appropriate), and don't forget a snack for yourself. Those waits can drag on. Bring an extra onesie in case of diaper disasters and a thin blanket for comfort in chilly offices. If your baby gets fussy post-shots, gentle rocking, a quick feed if allowed, or some silly faces can help calm things down. Sometimes just stepping outside for a minute after the appointment resets everyone's mood.

No two babies react the same way to checkups. Some take shots in stride; others act like it's the end of the world. Either way, try not to overthink it if you have a rough day at the clinic. You're not being judged on how calm or composed your kid is. You're there to keep them healthy and safe, and that's what counts.

Chapter Wrap-Up

Getting through all these health checks and vaccines isn't just about checking boxes; it's about being present, asking questions, and knowing when to push for more help. You've got what it takes to advocate for your child and support your partner through all the pokes and paperwork. Up next: balancing work demands with family life, because being there for your baby means figuring out how to juggle it all without losing yourself in the process.

CHAPTER 7

Work-Life Balance: Staying Present at Home and Work

Designing Your "Morning Launchpad" Routine

Mornings used to be simple: alarm, shower, coffee, out the door. Now, they can feel chaotic, you're juggling a baby, scanning work emails, chasing essentials, and navigating last-minute messes (like the cat's hallway surprise). This might not be the morning you imagined, but it's reality for many new dads.

You can't erase all the morning chaos, but you can make it manageable with a personalized routine. The key is to prioritize what's truly essential and skip the rest. Draw a line between what must get done, like changing the baby, prepping bottles, packing the diaper bag, and what can wait, such as ironing your shirt or scrolling through Instagram.

Keep your essentials list short: feed, change and dress baby, pack the bag, and gather your wallet, keys, and work badge. Anything beyond that is optional.

Efficiency doesn't mean sacrificing connection. Simple morning rituals can turn routines into bonding opportunities. For some, it's a quick "family snuggle" or a two-minute dance party with the kids. It doesn't have to be complex; the magic is in its consistency. A kiss for your partner or a silly song for your child can transform a frantic morning into a shared moment.

Preparing the night before is your best strategy for calmer mornings. Set out clothes for everyone, no early-morning digging for clean onesies. Prep bottles and snacks ahead; organize them in the fridge or by the door. Make sure the diaper bag has spare outfits and wipes (always pack a second onesie), and get your work bag ready, laptop, charger, headphones, whatever you need, so you're not scavenging through the house before your coffee kicks in.

On the topic of coffee, a programmable coffee maker is a lifesaver. Set it to brew before you get up so you're lured from bed by fresh coffee aroma. For breakfast, prep grab-

and-go options like overnight oats or egg muffins, easy to eat while managing a baby.

A dedicated "launchpad zone" at home streamlines departures. Whether it's a table by the door or a hallway shelf, give every essential a spot: bags, lunches, keys, water bottles, shoes. Keep a checklist handy if you're forgetful: "Diaper bag? Bottles? Coffee? Baby's toy?" A bit of organization upfront prevents headaches later.

Don't rush the morning handoff, whether it's to your partner, daycare, or a grandparent. Make these goodbyes meaningful, with a quick rhyme, secret handshake, or note—simple routines remind your child and partner they matter, even in the rush. For your partner, pause for a quick check-in: "Need anything from me?" or "Let's crush it today." These small moments build connection and teamwork.

Interactive Element: Morning Launchpad Checklist

- Set out tomorrow's clothes for everyone.
- Prep bottles/snacks and stash in fridge.
- Pack diaper bag with two outfits, wipes, and a pacifier.
- Load work bag with essentials.
- Place both bags in the launchpad zone near the door.
- Set the coffee maker timer.
- Write a quick checklist or reminder note.
- Decide on a morning ritual—a dance party, snuggle, or high-five.

Try this checklist for one week and adjust as needed until your mornings feel smoother.

By organizing and making space for quick moments of connection, you'll reduce the frantic searches, avoid forgotten items, and set everyone up for a better day.

Staying Connected After Paternity Leave

Returning to work after paternity leave can feel like a collision of two worlds. One minute, you're the go-to person for midnight feedings, baby burps, and surprise diaper blowouts. Next, you're back in meetings, emails, and lunchroom small talk, feeling like you've left half your heart at home.

Most dads I've talked to describe that first week back as a strange mix of relief, guilt, and sadness. You might even feel invisible; some coworkers are eager to hear "dad stories," but the pace of work hasn't slowed down for your adjustment. The anxiety is real: *Am I missing too much? Will my partner resent me for being out of the house? How do I stay involved when I'm not physically there?*

It's normal to miss your baby with a deep ache and still crave adult conversation and a break from baby talk. That doesn't make you a bad dad; it makes you human. One friend told me he spent his first lunch break hiding in his car, scrolling through baby photos and wondering if the baby would even remember him by the end of the week. Another dad confessed that seeing photos of his partner's "perfect" day on social media left him feeling left out and weirdly competitive, like he was missing the magic moments. These feelings often come in waves: pride for working hard, guilt for not being home, relief for small freedoms, and longing for baby snuggles.

Staying connected during the workday takes a little creativity. Scheduled photo or video updates are a simple way to bridge the gap. Ask your partner or caregiver to send you a daily pic or short clip, maybe after nap time or during lunch. Set an alarm as a reminder if needed. Even ten seconds of seeing your baby's face can reset your mood and remind you what you're working for. If your workplace allows it, take a lunch break and FaceTime or make a quick call home. It doesn't need to be long; even a minute or two can help you feel involved and let your partner know you're thinking about them. Some dads use their commute for voice memos, recording a silly message or song to be played for the baby later.

Advocating for flexibility at work might feel intimidating at first, but it's worth considering if your job allows any wiggle room. If you want to request remote days, flexible start times, or a phased return, plan what you'll say in advance. Here's an example: "I've really valued my time at home with my new child. To stay focused and productive at work while still supporting my family, I'd like to discuss the possibility of working from home one day a week (or adjusting my hours temporarily). I'm committed to meeting my responsibilities and believe this change will help me bring my best self to both roles." Most managers appreciate honest communication and clear plans. If remote work isn't possible, see if you can adjust your hours slightly to avoid traffic and maximize morning or evening family time.

Walking in the door after a long day can set the mood for your whole evening. It's easy to get sucked into checking messages or zoning out as soon as you drop your bag, but a quick "tech-off" ritual helps shift gears from work brain to dad brain. Try leaving your phone in another room for twenty minutes when you get home—just enough time to focus on your family before catching up on notifications. If you've had a particularly stressful day, take a five-minute decompression walk around the block or even just stand outside and take a few breaths before heading inside. This small pause can make you less snappy and more present.

Make the first moments at home count. Instead of rushing straight to chores or screens, greet your baby and partner with intention, maybe it's a "first hug goes to baby" rule or a silly "I'm home!" song that makes everyone laugh. Let your partner know you see them with eye contact and a genuine question about their day before diving into logistics or complaints. These habits tell your family they matter more than any lingering work stress.

Balancing work and family isn't about perfection; it's about showing up where you are, with whatever energy you have left. If you can't be physically present during the day, small actions keep you emotionally connected. Celebrate the wins: that lunch break video call, the silly voice memo, or the moment when your baby lights up at your arrival, even if it's just for ten minutes before dinner chaos begins. Your presence, even in these micro-bursts, shapes your bond more than any grand gesture. Over time, these rituals become anchors for both you and your family—reminders that while work is important, being present matters most.

There's no blueprint for finding equilibrium here. Every family is different, and every workplace has its quirks. But each intentional act, requesting flexibility, prioritizing connection over distraction, protecting those first moments at home, adds up. The days are busy and sometimes messy, but these choices help keep you right where you want to be: in the center of your child's life, even when you're pulled in every direction.

Maximizing Family Time in 10-Minute Windows

You might think you need whole afternoons or a free weekend to really connect with your baby, but real life rarely hands you those wide-open spaces. It's the micro-moments, the in-between slices of your day, that add up. Research on child development keeps coming back to this: kids thrive on quality, not just quantity. Your baby doesn't care how flashy the moment is; what matters most is your attention, even if it's just for ten focused minutes. The myth that only hours-long playdates build memories just isn't true. Those pint-sized bursts of connection, where you're engaged, present, and available, are the building blocks of trust and attachment.

Imagine you're home after work with a list of chores and a baby who's grumpy after a short nap. Instead of stressing about not having an hour to spare, look for your ten-minute window. Maybe you scoop up your little one, flop onto the living room rug, and start a silly sing-along. Your baby might not understand every word, but the rhythm, the sound of your voice, and the goofy faces will light them up. Or grab a board book and let your kid "help" turn the pages, making animal sounds at every picture. It's less about finishing the story and more about that shared laugh when you both moo like cows or roar like dinosaurs.

If you want a menu of ten-minute dad-and-baby activities to keep handy, here's a quick list: have a sock puppet storytime with two mismatched socks and some wild voices; shake out the wiggles with a morning dance party; crank up your favorite song and bounce around together; take a stroller or carrier stroll around the block, even if it's just to the corner and back; invent a silly face contest in front of the mirror, seeing who can make the baby giggle first; or hold an impromptu "parade" through the house banging wooden spoons on pots. You don't need fancy toys or Pinterest-worthy crafts to make magic. Your energy, even if you're tired, is what turns routine moments into memories.

Protecting these micro-windows in your day takes intention, but it's possible even on busy schedules. Block out ten minutes on your phone calendar and label it "Baby Break." Treat it like any other meeting. Set a recurring reminder for right after dinner or before bedtime so this time doesn't get swallowed by chores or screens. If you work from home or have odd hours, sandwich these moments between calls or emails—take a stretch break and roll a ball back and forth on the floor or play peekaboo behind your laptop. The trick isn't to find more time but to use what you have with total focus, no multitasking.

Sometimes the urge to check your phone creeps in, but resist it during these ten-minute bursts. Let notifications wait. Give your kid your eyes and your hands for just those minutes. Babies and toddlers are pros at sensing when you're only half-present. They want all of you, even for just one silly little block of time. That attention means more than any expensive gadget could.

If you're worried about not remembering these moments or want to see how they add up over time, consider starting a "Dad Win" mini-journal or photo log. After each micro-activity, snap a quick selfie with your kid—maybe both of you covered in drool after raspberry blowing or sporting wild hair from dance time. These photos become proof that connection isn't about perfection; it's about presence. If journaling feels daunting, keep it simple: jot down one sentence each night describing your favorite mini-moment from the day ("Today we played monster parade in the kitchen, and baby shrieked with laughter"). Some dads share their high point and low point of the day with their partner after bedtime, a quick check-in that makes both of you feel seen.

The power of reflection can't be overstated here. Looking back at your mini-journal or scrolling through those goofy selfies will remind you that even during weeks packed with work stress or sleepless nights, you found time for joy. You built connection in small doses, ten minutes at a time. There's no scorecard for who did it best, but there's immense value in knowing these micro-moments are shaping your child's sense of security and their view of you as present and loving.

The beauty of these short windows is that they're flexible. If one day goes sideways and you miss your moment, just find another tomorrow. No guilt required. You're teaching your child that love doesn't wait for big events, it lives in the quick, everyday bursts that fill their world with laughter and safety.

Dad Guilt: Letting Go of Perfection and Comparison

Dad guilt creeps in quietly. You think you're just tired from work, but suddenly you catch yourself wondering if you're doing enough—at home, with your kid, for your partner. Maybe you scrolled past a post of a dad baking homemade muffins after running a half marathon and helping with math homework, all before noon. It's ridiculous, yet you feel a pang in your chest. Why can't I keep up? Social media is a highlight reel and, let's be honest, nobody posts about the nights they lost it or served frozen pizza three days in a row. Still, the pressure is real. Everyone seems to be winning at this dad thing, except you, right? It's easy to believe the myth of the "super-parent," that you should always be productive, patient, and perfectly present, no matter what.

Cultural expectations pile on top. There's this unspoken script that says you should be crushing it at work while also being emotionally tuned in, physically present, and always available at home. Cue the guilt when you fall short in either direction. Miss a bedtime because of late meetings? Guilt. Snap at your partner after a long day? More guilt. And when tension builds between work deadlines and family needs, you end up feeling like you're failing everywhere—never quite enough anywhere. That's the mental trap so many dads fall into: thinking you're the only one who drops the ball sometimes.

The first thing that helps is recognizing when unrealistic standards have snuck in. Sometimes it takes stepping back for a reality check. Here's an exercise that works: Write down what's actually in your control today and what isn't. You can't control the baby's sleep schedule or surprise work emergencies. You can control how you respond to stress or if you say yes to another project when your plate is full. Ask yourself, *"What would I tell my best friend if he was in my shoes?"* Odds are, you'd give him a break, remind him he's doing his best, and maybe even crack a joke about survival being enough some days.

There's real freedom in picking your battles, choosing what matters most right now, and letting the rest slide without shame. On days when everything feels like too much, focus on just three things that are most important. Maybe it's making your baby laugh, having a real conversation with your partner, and finishing that urgent work task. Circle those three and let everything else, the dishes, unread emails, over-the-top playdates, sit on the back burner for now. This isn't laziness; it's survival with intention. When someone asks for help or an invitation pops up, try saying, "I can't this time," or "Not today." No explanation required. Protecting your bandwidth is self-care.

Here's something I wish every new dad could see: Even the days that go sideways can still be good ones. There was this one Thursday when nothing went according to plan. The baby woke screaming from a nap just as I dialed into a meeting. Lunch turned into a handful of crackers scavenged between diaper changes and spilled milk. My partner and I snapped at each other over whose turn it was to take out the trash. I felt like I'd lost at both work and home before 2 p.m.

But then, while sitting on the floor in mismatched socks and a stained shirt, I started making faces at my daughter just to break the tension. She cracked up, drool running down her chin, and suddenly, everything else faded out for a minute.

That laugh didn't erase my stress or magically finish my to-do list, but it mattered more than any perfect plan.

Some of my favorite memories as a dad didn't look impressive from the outside. They weren't Instagram-worthy: just me and my son sitting on the porch in the rain, sharing soggy crackers; me letting my kid "help" fold laundry by wearing every sock on his arms; watching cartoons together when I was too fried to play pretend. Those moments felt real, imperfect but honest. They're the ones I remember most when I'm tempted to measure myself against someone else's filtered story.

Dad guilt loves to whisper that you're not enough unless you juggle everything flawlessly. That's not true. Your kid cares about how you show up, not what you get done or how others see it. If all you can do some days is be there, even if tired or distracted, you're still enough. Permission granted to drop the cape, skip perfection, and just be present for the mess and magic alike.

Managing Work Stress Without Bringing It Home

Work stress is sneaky. It follows you, clings to your shoulders like an invisible backpack, and before you know it, that pressure from the day seeps into your life at home. You might notice you're short-tempered as soon as you walk through the door, snapping at your partner over nothing, rolling your eyes at the baby's fuss, or feeling totally checked out even when you're sitting right there on the living room floor. Sometimes it's not obvious at first. Maybe you find yourself staring off into space, not really hearing the questions your partner asks, or scrolling through your phone while your kid tugs on your pant leg. Mood shifts can be subtle: a sigh that's a little too heavy, a one-word answer where you'd usually tell a story, or that feeling of being stuck in two places at once—your body at home, your mind still tangled in emails and deadlines.

The trouble is, if you let that stress tag along every day, it builds up. Suddenly, small annoyances explode into arguments over who forgot to buy wipes or whose turn it is to handle bedtime. You might start feeling like you're failing as a dad or partner, when really, you're just carrying too much from work into the house. The first trick is spotting the early signs: irritability right after getting home, zoning out during dinner, or feeling waves of frustration out of proportion to what's actually happening. If you start to feel like the world's worst version of yourself for no apparent reason, pause and check if work followed you home.

Transition rituals help break this spell. Think of them as a mental "costume change." Even if you work from home, it makes a difference. Change into comfy clothes as soon as you clock out; the physical swap signals your brain it's time to shift gears. If you commute by car or train, take five slow breaths before walking inside—inhale for four seconds, exhale for six, let your mind clear for just a moment. Some dads swear by walking around the block before entering the house, using the time to shake off meetings and reset their focus. If you're coming from a stressful day in the kitchen, bathroom, or bedroom "office," close your laptop with intention, stand up, stretch, and shake it off for sixty seconds before stepping back into family mode.

Talking about work stress with your partner is vital, but there's a fine line between healthy sharing and letting it flood the evening. The "headline and feelings" method works wonders: give a quick summary like "Tough day, boss dumped a new project on me," then add how you feel about it, "I'm annoyed but glad to be done." Then move on. This way, your partner knows what's going on without feeling like they have to fix it or absorb all of your stress. Set boundaries for venting: maybe agree on five or ten minutes of "work talk," then switch topics. If you find yourself spiraling or getting heated again later in the night, remind yourself, "Headline only," and save the deep dive for another time or a different friend who gets the grind.

Self-compassion is key here. Some days will be rough; that doesn't make you a bad dad. Quick stress reduction practices can do wonders and don't require carving out a whole hour alone. Family walks after dinner are simple but powerful— moving together gets everyone fresh air and burns off leftover tension from the day. Don't underestimate the power of a short gratitude roundtable at dinner: each person (even if it's just you and your partner) shares one thing that went well or made them smile. This isn't about pretending everything's perfect; it's about rewiring your brain to see good moments even in messy days.

One of my favorite tricks is what I call the "3-minute driveway reset." Before I step inside, whether I'm coming home from work or just done with chores, I sit in the car with no music and no phone. I roll my shoulders back, take three deep breaths, and remind myself that whatever happened at work stays outside those walls. Sometimes I picture myself leaving all my stress in the glove compartment. Then I go inside, ready to greet my family as dad, not as an overworked employee.

All these strategies take practice. You'll mess up sometimes, you'll still bark at someone or zone out mid-conversation, but having these small rituals in place gives you a way back to center. When you show up, present and unburdened (or at least trying), everyone feels it. Your kid doesn't need perfection; they need to see you make the effort to be there with them, even when work has been brutal. That effort, those transition moments, those resets, matter more than any grand gesture or apology later on.

The Dad and Partner Check-In: Keeping Your Team Strong

Relationships in the first year after a baby arrives are tested in ways few expect. It's not just sleepless nights or endless chores; it's the subtle disconnect that can happen as you both power through survival mode. Regular check-ins with your partner are essential to prevent drifting apart. These aren't exhaustive problem-solving sessions or logistical meetings. They're simple opportunities to see each other, voice frustrations before they build up, and stay in sync as a parenting team. If you feel like ships passing in the night, check-ins can bring you back together.

Finding time is tough, but it pays off. Try weekly or bi-weekly "state of the union" chats to keep communication open. Fifteen minutes after bedtime or a quiet coffee while the baby naps can make a difference. These moments don't have to be formal; a chat on the porch or a walk with the stroller works. What's crucial is showing up intentionally, not just as household managers, but as co-captains of your family.

A structure keeps things productive and relaxed. Three prompts help: "What's working?" "What's tough?" and "What could we try differently?" This focus prevents blame or old fights from resurfacing. Truly listen to your partner's answers, don't interrupt or rush to fix things. Sometimes all that's needed is acknowledgment: "Yeah, that's been hard." Share your own wins and struggles honestly as well. If you're stretched thin or unsure how to help, say so. The goal isn't perfection, but connection.

Appreciation holds everything together. Don't just dwell on negatives; call out the small things your partner did well, whether it's being patient at 3 a.m. or handling a meltdown at the store. Positive feedback isn't cheesy; it keeps you both going.

Check-ins don't need to look the same every time. Catch up while walking, texting, or sharing takeout after bedtime. For extra-busy days, a quick "How are you really doing?" text or shared notebook entry keeps the door open. If sitting down together feels too hard, even a brief voice memo helps.

Real life interrupts. Fatigue gets the better of you. Sometimes you'll miss a week or end up arguing. That's normal, don't let it stop you. Try using a phrase like, "Can we pause and come back to this tomorrow?" or "I love you, even if I'm grumpy." Resetting doesn't mean avoiding problems, but making space for repair.

Low-pressure talks are sustainable. If you're tired, keep it short: "What's one thing that worked for us this week?" Or ask directly, "What do you need from me right now?" Always end on something positive, a thank you, a high-five, or a laugh about some parenting mishap. Even when things are chaotic, celebrating one "dad win" (or "team win") can shift your mindset and remind you why you're doing this together.

Scheduling regular check-ins builds trust and teamwork, even in the chaos. You'll spot patterns before resentment sets in, and feel less isolated. These check-ins aren't just for venting; they help you celebrate wins, brainstorm small adjustments, and remember you're partners as well as parents.

Quick Check-In Template

- What's working this week?
- What's been tough?
- What could we try differently next week?
- Anything you want to appreciate about each other?
- End with a team win or a laugh.

Don't stress if some weeks are clunky or interrupted by the baby or work. What matters is that you keep showing up, making adjustments, and giving your relationship space to grow.

In the end, this chapter isn't about perfect balance; it's about staying genuinely connected through messy, real effort. You won't always get it right, but building habits of presence, teamwork, and honest conversation will help you navigate the wild first year. Next up: we'll dive into money, gear, and growing together as a family, so you can feel ready for whatever comes next.

CHAPTER 8

Money, Gear, and Growing as a Family

Budget Reality Check: What You Really Need (and What's Hype)

The first time I saw a "baby registry must-haves" list, I laughed, and then panicked. You might know the feeling: standing in a store, overwhelmed by shelves of gear promising to make you a better parent and your baby safer or happier. Most of us want to give our kids everything, but there's a big difference between what's truly needed and what's just clever marketing. This distinction is easy to lose track of, especially when you're exhausted and anxious to do things right.

Let's get honest about the actual costs. The first year with a baby can be expensive, but it doesn't have to break the bank. Most new parents spend $200–$400 per month. Diapers and wipes alone cost about $50–$80 monthly if you use disposables. Formula can add $80–$150 more per month if

166

you're not exclusively breastfeeding. Basic clothing costs about $20–$40 a month, given growth spurts and inevitable messes. Pediatrician visits sneak up, even with good insurance, you'll want to budget $20–$50 each month for these.

There are always hidden expenses. Babies create mountains of laundry, so expect to buy more detergent and pay higher utility bills from extra washing. Cleaning supplies, gentle soaps, disinfectant wipes, suddenly become household staples. Even your heating or cooling bills may rise as you try to keep your baby comfortable. Nightlights, white noise machines, and other little things add up, so count on $30–$50 more monthly for these "invisible" categories.

So what's worth your money? Start with an honest "must-have" versus "nice-to-have" list. Essentials are a safe, *new* car seat, a crib or bassinet that meets safety standards, and a reliable thermometer. You'll want five to seven simple onesies, two sleep sacks or swaddles (if recommended for non-rollers), a practical baby bathtub, a few bottles (even if breastfeeding), and a pack of burp cloths. Skip extras like wipe warmers (they cool fast), and designer shoes or fancy outfits (babies outgrow them quickly and can't walk). Wait on swings, bouncers, or high chairs until you know what your baby likes; not every child cares about gadgets.

Don't tackle your baby budget alone. Community swaps and "buy nothing" groups are treasure troves for gently used baby gear, clothes, and toys, especially things only needed for a short window. Borrowing from friends or family is common and welcomed; most are glad to pass things along, and you'll do the same one day. Consignment shops are smart if you need strollers, carriers, or bouncers; you can find like-new gear for much less. When in doubt, just ask: "Do you have any baby stuff you're done with?" People are usually relieved to declutter.

Here are a couple of real-world examples. Josh and his partner managed on a tight $50/month baby budget by using cloth diapers, hand-me-down clothes, and a borrowed bassinet. Their splurges were a new car seat and quality bottles. Another friend with twins spent closer to $150/month because of formula and double sets of essentials, but saved by joining local swap groups for toys and clothes.

Sample "bare-bones" monthly budget for a family of three:

- Diapers and wipes: $60
- Formula/Breastfeeding accessories: $100
- Basic clothes: $25
- Medical copays: $30
- Laundry/cleaning: $20
- **Total:** $235/month

If your situation allows wiggle room to splurge, pick your battles. A comfy carrier or blackout curtains can make life easier.

Interactive Element: Quick "Must-Have vs. Hype" Checklist

- Safe car seat (new): Must-have
- Crib/bassinet: Must-have
- Five+ onesies: Must-have
- Thermometer: Must-have
- Baby bathtub: Must-have
- Swings/bouncers: Wait and see
- Wipe warmer: Skip it
- Designer outfits/shoes: Skip it
- High chair: Wait until solids

- Changing table: Nice-to-have (a sturdy surface works too)
- White noise machine: Nice-to-have if it helps sleep.

As your child grows, your priorities will shift, and you'll learn what actually helps. Don't let social media or marketing pressure you; your baby really just needs you a lot more than any gadget.

Navigating Insurance, Paperwork, and Financial Surprises

Adding a new baby to your health insurance feels like a game of beat-the-clock, especially when you're running on zero sleep. Hospitals hand you forms while you're still in a daze. Bills trickle in weeks later, just when you think you're catching up. The clock starts ticking the minute your baby arrives. Most insurance companies give you 30 days, sometimes 60, to get your child added to your policy. Miss that window and you might be stuck waiting months for open enrollment or paying out of pocket for every tiny cough and checkup.

As soon as you have that birth certificate, reach out to your employer's HR or your insurance provider, even if you're still living in pajamas. Ask them straight: "What's my deadline for adding my baby?" and "What documents do I need?" It's worth getting crystal clear on deductibles, copays, and what counts as an in-network provider. Sometimes, a pediatrician you met in the hospital isn't covered by your plan, and surprise bills can spiral from there.

Paperwork is relentless in the first year. You'll need to order your baby's birth certificate, usually from the hospital or your state's vital records office. Next comes the Social Security application, which many hospitals can submit for you. If not, you'll have to do it at the local office or by mail, and you'll need that number for everything from insurance to tax returns. Pediatrician offices want copies of both, along with your insurance card, before the first well-baby visit. Make a digital folder: scan these documents, save them to a password-protected spot (like cloud storage), and keep paper copies in a fire-safe box or locked drawer. Store immunization records and visit summaries there too. When the daycare paperwork starts rolling in, you'll thank yourself for being organized.

You'll get hit with unexpected costs; nobody warns you how fast they add up. Maybe your baby spikes a fever on a weekend and you end up at urgent care, only to find out they're out-of-network. That bill arrives, and it's way more than you expected. Or maybe there's a prescription that isn't fully covered, or a specialist visit for something minor that insurance only partially pays for. Then there are those extra childcare hours when work runs late or your sitter cancels last minute. Some expenses are just impossible to predict: extra formula when breastfeeding gets tricky, or backup glasses after a pair gets snapped in half during tummy time. You can't plan for everything, but building an emergency fund, just $20–$30 tucked away each month, can soften the blow when these surprises hit.

Communicating with insurance companies and HR departments can feel like decoding ancient scripts. When you write an email, be direct: "Hi, I just had a baby and need to add them to my health insurance policy. Can you confirm the steps and documents required? Is there a specific deadline?" If something doesn't make sense on a bill, don't hesitate to call or email back: "Can you explain this charge? Was this provider in-network? Is there any way to appeal this amount?" Keep every reply in your digital folder—screenshots, PDFs, even photos of paperwork if needed.

Organizing bills is half the battle. Use a simple spreadsheet or calendar app to log what's due, what you've paid, and what's still outstanding. List the date of service, provider, billed amount, what insurance paid, and what's left for you. This makes it easier to spot mistakes or overcharges. If you catch an error (and they happen often), call billing right away: "I believe there may be a mistake on this bill. Can we review it together?" Document every conversation: who you spoke with, the date, and any reference numbers.

Templates and Trackers

For insurance questions: Subject: Adding Newborn to Health Insurance
Hi [HR/Provider Name],

I recently welcomed a new baby and need to add them to my health insurance plan. Could you please confirm what steps I should take and which documents are required? Also, what is the deadline for this process?

Thank you!

[Your Name]

For bill tracking:

Date	Provider	Billed	Insurance Paid	You Owe	Paid?	Notes
6/10	Dr. Smith	$150	$120	$30	Yes	Well check

Keep this tracker on your phone or computer and update it after every bill.

When contesting a bill: "Hi [Billing Department], I have a question regarding this charge from [date]. According to my insurance statement, this should be covered at [percentage]. Can we review this together and check for errors? Please let me know if any additional paperwork is needed from my end."

You'll never remember every detail in the fog of new parenthood, but having steps written down and using scripts when nerves hit makes things less overwhelming. You don't need to become an accountant overnight; you just need a system that lets you breathe a little easier when life gets chaotic.

Choosing Baby Gear Without Overspending

Staring at walls of baby gear, strollers, car seats, swings, gadgets with more buttons than a spaceship, can make your head spin. It's easy to get pulled into the "more is better" trap when you see the endless Instagram reels and unboxing videos showing shiny, color-coordinated nurseries. The truth is, most of that stuff collects dust or gets dumped in a closet as fast as your kid outgrows a onesie. What matters is picking gear that's actually safe, works for your day-to-day, and doesn't leave you regretting every swipe of your credit card.

Start with safety. Before spending a dime, check the latest safety ratings for any big-ticket items: car seats, cribs, high chairs. The Consumer Product Safety Commission website lists recent recalls and safety standards, so you can be sure you're not buying something with a hidden hazard. Look for clear labels, simple harnesses, and sturdy construction. Don't skip this step. Never trust only online reviews or marketing hype; those five-star ratings might come from folks who never crash-tested a car seat in a real accident or tried to wrangle a screaming baby into a tricky harness at 3 a.m. When possible, "test-drive" strollers and car seats in-store. Snap the buckles, fold them up, lift them with one arm, see if they fit your car trunk or your actual strength level. You'll thank yourself the first time you have to pop open a stroller one-handed while holding coffee and wrangling a diaper bag.

When it comes to buying, borrowing, or waiting, use a simple decision matrix. Car seats and crib mattresses are two things worth buying new if possible. Safety standards change fast, and used items may be expired or have hidden damage. Things like baby swings, bouncers, and most newborn clothes can easily be borrowed from friends or snagged secondhand. Babies often use these for just a few months before moving on, so there's no shame in passing them along. Wait on gadgets like bottle warmers or wipe dispensers until you know if your baby even cares. They may just want warm cuddles, not warm wipes.

Trading gear with friends or through community groups works wonders if you know what to look for. Inspect everything closely before bringing it home. Moldy spots on fabric? Skip it. Cracked plastic or missing screws? Not worth the risk. Car seats have clear expiration dates stamped on the bottom. Never use one past its date or after an accident. High chairs and strollers should open and close smoothly without pinching fingers or catching fabric. For clothes and carriers, check seams, snaps, and zippers for wear—babies are tough on gear but also sensitive to rough edges.

It's so easy to get swept up in marketing pressure, especially after seeing those "must-have" lists on social feeds or hearing stories about miracle products that "change everything." Most of that is just clever advertising designed to give you FOMO (fear of missing out). Focus on what works for your family's actual lifestyle instead of what looks good in a photo grid. Some families swear by high-end bassinets that rock themselves; others find their baby sleeps best in their arms or a basic crib. Think about your space, your routine, and your actual hands-on needs.

To help filter out the noise, list out your family's top three most-used baby items after a month or two. For us, it was a sturdy travel stroller (lightweight enough for subway steps), a soft wrap carrier (perfect for walks and soothing fussy evenings), and an easy-to-clean bouncer (lifesaver during solo showers). Everything else we thought we needed ended up in the closet or was donated. Ask other dads what they really use, and most will tell you the same thing: the simpler, the better.

When well-meaning friends or relatives offer gifts that don't fit your space or values, respond kindly but honestly: "Thanks so much! We're all set for now, but I'll let you know if we need anything." This simple script keeps things positive without cluttering your life with stuff you don't want or need.

Gear Swap Checklist

When swapping gear with friends or through local groups, keep this list handy:

- Check fabric for stains or mold.
- Test all buckles/snaps/zippers.
- Inspect for missing screws/parts.
- For car seats: confirm expiration date/sticker intact.
- Ask about recalls—search model numbers online.
- Wipe down surfaces before using.
- Ensure no rough edges or fraying straps.
- Trust your gut: if something feels off, pass.

Selecting baby gear doesn't mean assembling a miniature version of Babies 'R' Us in your living room. It means choosing only what truly fits your life right now and letting go of the rest, no guilt required. Your baby will remember your arms and your laughter long after they forget the brand of their first stroller.

Monthly "Dad Wins" Reflection Pages: Tracking Growth and Gratitude

There's something quietly powerful about pausing to notice the moments that would otherwise slip by. In the chaos of new fatherhood, it's so easy to focus on what you didn't do, what you forgot, or the hundred things still on your mental checklist. But if you take a few minutes every month to jot down your "dad wins," big or small, you'll start to see your own story in a whole new way. Maybe you figured out how to calm your baby's colic with your favorite playlist, or you managed to get through a rough week at work without snapping at home. Maybe you just survived a week of teething and still managed to make your partner laugh. That counts. These little victories are the glue holding this wild year together.

Try using simple prompts as anchors. Ask yourself, "What did I do well this month?" Don't be shy. Brag a little. Did you finally nail the baby carrier after a week of wrestling with straps? Did you handle the 3 a.m. fever without losing your cool? Write it down. Pick your favorite memory with your baby, maybe it was their first smile, a spontaneous giggle fit, or just a quiet morning snuggle. These are the moments that tend to fade if you don't capture them. Sometimes it's not about milestones but about a feeling: pride after handling bedtime solo, or relief after getting everyone to sleep before midnight for once.

It helps to split your reflection into two sides: practical achievements and emotional milestones. On one side, list out what you actually did—changed every diaper, cooked a meal, survived an outing with no forgotten items. On the other side, go deeper: "What was the biggest challenge I faced and how did I get through it?" Maybe it was balancing work deadlines with family needs or managing your own frustration when nothing seemed to work. Then, "What did I discover about my baby or my partner this month?"

Perhaps you noticed your baby loves silly faces more than fancy toys, or you saw how much your partner values small gestures like a surprise coffee or a quiet hug.

Make this check-in a ritual, not a chore. Some dads like to spend ten minutes alone at the end of each month, grab your phone or a notebook, and just let it flow. Others turn it into a family thing, sharing highlights and gratitude over dinner or during a quiet walk. If you're parenting with a partner, try trading reflections. Sometimes seeing yourself through their eyes reveals strengths you didn't notice. Don't worry about perfect sentences or spelling; what matters is honesty and showing up for yourself.

Over time, these reflection pages become more than just scribbles; they're proof of growth and resilience. When you're in the weeds on a hard day, flipping back to see how far you've come can be the reset your brain needs. You'll remember the first time you soothed your baby alone, or that night you figured out how to get everyone to sleep (even if only for three hours). That sense of progress matters. It builds confidence and keeps doubt from taking over.

I've heard from dads who started this ritual, unsure if it would help. One dad told me he filled out his first page thinking he'd only write "kept baby alive." But after reading back months later, he found stories he'd forgotten—a rainy Saturday spent building blanket forts, the moment his daughter reached for his hand for the first time, a hard conversation with his partner that made things better. Another dad said his monthly notes turned into bedtime stories for his toddler later on, which became their favorite end-of-day ritual.

You don't need fancy journals or apps—scraps of paper, voice memos, even text messages to yourself will do. Just keep them somewhere safe. If you want to get creative, add photos or draw doodles next to each win. Invite your partner or even older kids into the ritual as they grow; gratitude and self-recognition aren't just for babies and dads, they strengthen the whole family.

Below is a simple template to use each month:

Dad Wins Reflection Template

- What did I do well this month?
- Favorite memory with my baby:
- Biggest challenge I faced and how I handled it:
- Something new I learned about my baby or partner:

- What am I grateful for right now?

No matter how messy life gets (and it will), this practice grounds you in what's real, your effort, your presence, and the everyday magic that comes from showing up again and again.

Building Family Traditions from Year One

In the early days of parenting, it's easy to overlook how much you're shaping your family's story. Traditions aren't about grand gestures or expensive gifts; they're about the everyday rhythms, quirks, and small rituals that give your family its unique character. When you start these routines early, even if your baby isn't aware yet, you're planting the seeds for belonging and togetherness. Simple routines like Sunday pancakes or reading a favorite silly bedtime story with voices that change each month might seem minor, but they become treasured childhood memories and the backbone of your family's identity.

Marking milestones creates a shared, unique timeline. Monthly "birthday" photos with the same toy or chair provide a visual record of growth and time together. First holidays become opportunities to invent new rituals, maybe a single handmade ornament for baby's first winter holiday, a family selfie each New Year's morning, or a handprint turkey for Thanksgiving. These repeated moments matter. The routine itself brings comfort, even when no one recalls how it started.

Traditions don't have to be time-consuming or costly; flexible and simple ones often stick best, fitting easily into busy lives. Maybe after dinner, you always take a brief family walk, even around the block in bad weather. Perhaps Friday nights become impromptu dance parties, regardless of energy or coordination. You could write your baby an annual letter summarizing their year and your hopes, saving it for them to read someday. Skip store-bought holiday décor and instead make crafts together, letting your child's scribbles take center stage on the fridge.

The most meaningful rituals are those created together. If you're parenting with a partner, find a quiet moment to discuss the kind of traditions you'd like. Reflect on what you enjoyed or disliked about your own childhood customs, and consider trying something new—a special birthday breakfast, a funny phrase before leaving the house, or a quirky new holiday routine. Don't hesitate to let go of anything that feels forced. Traditions should be about building connection, not striving for perfection. Even if your child is too young to fully understand, they'll sense the warmth and safety these routines provide.

Stories from other dads highlight the power of traditions, especially during tough times. One father started "Saturday Superhero Breakfasts," where everyone wore capes (old towels) while eating pancakes, which became a weekly anchor for both him and his son during stressful periods. Another dad wrote monthly birthday notes to his daughter, a short snapshot of her growth, which became an emotional family tradition as she got older.

Some families lean on rituals to weather hard days: making popcorn and watching old cartoons when someone's had a rough week, or lighting a candle before dinner and sharing one good thing about the day. These aren't dramatic or social-media-worthy, but their ordinariness makes them powerful, weaving everyone together. Kids latch onto all sorts of little things—a favorite song for car rides, silly nicknames only used at home, or always sitting in the same spot for storytime. Over the years, these details become part of the family's identity.

To get started, brainstorm together. Even if your partner seems uninterested or your baby is too little to participate, list five comforting or joyful things you already do (bedtime snuggles, funny morning greetings, stroller walks). Make one "official" or invent something new, like silly hat dinners once a month or simple backyard picnics every weekend. Adapt or change traditions as your family grows and interests change.

No two families will have the same rituals, and that uniqueness is what makes traditions special. Whether you're making pancakes in superhero capes or taking monthly photos in the same chair, you're building comforting rituals and a safety net of memories that will hold your family close through whatever comes next.

Spotlight Stories: Dads Redefining Fatherhood in Diverse Families

Every family has its own rhythm, and sometimes that rhythm means rewriting the rulebook. I've talked with dads from all walks of life, and what stands out is how each found a way to shape parenthood to fit their reality, not someone else's. Take Marcus, who never imagined raising his son alone but now calls his tight-knit apartment building "the village." When a friend's baby outgrew her crib, it landed in Marcus's living room before he even asked. He started doing toy swaps with neighbors, sharing books, clothes, and sometimes even splitting the cost for bigger gear. "We don't compete to have the fanciest stuff," Marcus told me. "We just make sure every kid has what they need, when they need it." He keeps a group text with single dads in his block, and they've become each other's backup for late-night runs or last-minute babysitting.

For Aaron and Leo, two dads who grew their family through adoption, the logistics were their biggest hurdle. They spent months sorting paperwork and even more time figuring out what gear would actually serve them as new parents. Instead of buying everything new, they reached out on local

187

parenting forums and quickly discovered a network of LGBTQ+ families ready to share advice and gently used essentials. Their most creative move was hosting a "bring your favorite baby item" potluck, a gathering where friends brought food and hand-me-downs. They learned quickly that a supportive community goes further than any store credit card. Holidays became their time to blend traditions: one year, they set up a menorah next to a rainbow sock garland and started a yearly family photo in silly hats. These small rituals helped their daughter feel surrounded by love—messy, colorful, and always genuine.

Blended families face their own set of puzzles. Jamal, stepdad to two kids and now dad to a newborn, found himself learning fast how to juggle different needs and backgrounds. His crew includes his partner's parents, who moved in to help with childcare, bringing their own customs and routines into the mix. Instead of fighting for control, Jamal leaned into flexibility. Family meetings at the kitchen table became a staple; everyone got a say in everything from meal planning to chore schedules. Hand-me-downs from older siblings were celebrated. His toddler wears her brother's superhero cape while crawling under the dining table. When his in-laws introduced their favorite lullabies from another country, Jamal realized his kids were growing up with a blend of languages and stories that made their home richer.

Some dads get creative with space and money out of necessity. Raj built his son's nursery corner using cinder blocks, leftover paint, and secondhand finds from an online free group. He focused on what mattered: safe sleep space, soft lighting, and a shelf for favorite books. Decorations came from family art sessions—handprints on the wall, paper stars hung from the ceiling. Neighbors pitched in with extra storage bins or outgrown toys. That room became a patchwork of gifts and DIY fixes, but Raj says it feels more special than anything he could've bought.

Celebrating wins looks different in every home. In multigenerational families like Sofia's, where grandpa moves in and cousins drop by often, "win" might mean everyone sitting around the table for Sunday soup or surviving a week of shared colds without losing patience. Some dads join online dad groups or meet at playgrounds for monthly "dad huddles." A place to laugh about bottle mishaps or brainstorm how to split costs on big purchases. Others keep group chats alive with photos of first steps, silly faces at dinner, or just a quick check-in after a rough night.

Community anchors these stories. Whether it's a chosen family of friends, neighbors-turned-co-parents, or relatives who step in as needed, support networks grow organically around the real needs of dads and kids. Rituals evolve naturally: group birthday parties in the park where everyone brings snacks and shares supplies; video calls with faraway relatives to keep ties strong; or simply finding pride in solving everyday problems as a team.

Looking at these stories reminds me that there's no single blueprint for being "the right kind" of dad. What matters is finding your crew, however you define it, and building something real together. Whether you're co-parenting across households or gathering your people for backyard cookouts, inclusion and creativity beat any catalog-perfect nursery.

As this book draws to a close, remember: families are built on resourcefulness and connection far more than on stuff or structure. Every dad's journey looks different, but what unites all great fathers is the courage to keep showing up with love, creativity, and a willingness to learn along the way. You don't need the newest gear or a perfect plan; you need presence, patience, and heart. The stories of diverse dads remind us that there is always another way forward, one that reflects who you are and the family you are building. So take a breath, trust your instincts, and know that you already have what it takes to lead with love. Because in the end, it is not the things you buy or the plans you make, it is the way you show up that makes you the hero your child is counting on.

CONCLUSION

Y ou made it. If you're reading this, you've survived sleepless nights, exploded diapers, baby meltdowns, and maybe even a few of your own. You've held a tiny human at 3 a.m. and wondered if you were doing anything right. But here's the truth: You are. That's not just fluff. I wrote this book because I know, deep in my bones, that dads like you don't get told that enough.

Let's circle back to why you picked up this guide in the first place. You wanted answers, sure. But more than that, you wanted to feel capable. Maybe you needed permission to step up and get in the game, or just someone to say, "Hey, you're not alone, and you're already nailing it more than you realize." That's the heart of this book. My mission was to hand you real tools, honest stories, and a big, friendly shove toward confidence. You can do this. You are vital. Your presence matters more than any perfect technique, gadget, or Instagram-worthy family photo.

So, what did we cover? A lot. We kicked things off with the wild tornado of the first 24 hours—panic, poop, and all. You learned to create a safe baby zone, set up a "dad launchpad," and use checklists so your sleep-deprived brain doesn't have to freestyle at 2 a.m. We talked about cluster feeding, tag-teaming with your partner, and the true meaning of "Dad Mode." It's not about being flawless, it's about showing up.

Then, you dove into hands-on baby care. Bottles, burping, baths, blowouts (yes, plural), and safe sleep without swaddling. You got practical hacks: keep supplies everywhere, laugh off disasters, and always have a backup shirt for yourself. We hammered home that you don't have to be an expert to be effective; action and effort matter most.

You built bonds, one ordinary moment at a time. Holding your baby close, skin-to-skin, singing off-key lullabies, inventing silly games, and making routines that are yours. We ditched the myth that connection has to be movie-magic. Real bonding grows from small, daily bits of effort: tummy time here, bedtime story there, a giggle that makes the whole hard week worth it.

Supporting your partner? We went there, too. You learned to spot the signs of postpartum struggle, offer empathy instead of fixing, and share the load at night. We talked real communication—awkward, honest, important. You became the kind of partner who takes action, not just instructions.

Teamwork isn't about tallying chores. It's about getting through the fog together, laughing at the mess, and forgiving each other (and yourself) when things get tense.

We didn't forget about you, either. Dad health matters. You learned to spot stress, use micro self-care breaks, and reach out when things get tough. You made space for your own feelings, without shame or apology, and found ways to connect with other dads. You discovered that "dad bod" isn't a punchline; it's a badge of hands-on parenting.

You learned to track milestones without losing your mind. You found out what's normal, what's not, and how to trust your gut when something feels off. You got scripts for talking to doctors, checklists for emergencies, and a reminder that every baby's timeline is unique.

We tackled work-life chaos. You built a "morning launchpad," figured out how to stay connected after paternity leave, and learned that ten-minute windows of real presence beat hours of distracted multitasking. You ditched the guilt, stopped comparing, and found ways to keep your partnership strong through check-ins and shared wins.

Money and gear? We pulled back the curtain on what's actually necessary and what's just hype. You got budgeting tips, insurance scripts, and a reality check on what matters. Your baby doesn't need a wipe warmer; they need you. And you've got this.

One thing I hope came through loud and clear: This book is for all dads. It's for the dad in sweats, the dad in a suit, the single dad, the dad with two dads, the adoptive dad, the dad who became a parent at 19, and the dad who started at 49. There's no "right" shape for a family. There's just showing up. No stereotypes, no shame, no gatekeeping. You belong here.

Let's recap some of the biggest "dad wins" you're taking with you:

- Daily care checklists that keep you sane.
- Dad hacks for chaos—like prepping stations and backup onesies.
- Teamwork rituals with your partner.
- Micro self-care routines (yes, five minutes counts).
- Milestone trackers you'll actually use.
- Creative family traditions, even if it's just Saturday pancakes or goofy bedtime handshakes.

If you remember nothing else, remember this: Progress beats perfection. Every day you show up, every time you try again, every time you laugh off a fail and try a new way, you're giving your child what they need most. You.

Keep using those reflection pages. Mark down your "dad wins" each month, no matter how small. Track milestones, not to compare, but to remember how far you and your family have come. Keep having those check-ins with your partner. Build traditions that reflect your real life, not someone else's highlight reel.

And don't keep this journey to yourself. Put the advice in this book to work. Try something new tonight. Reach out to a friend or a dad group. Ask for help when you need it. Share your stories, your real stories, the messy ones and the hilarious ones, with other dads. You'll inspire more people than you know.

If you hit a wall or you need backup, turn to the resources at the end of this book. There are helplines, online groups, and a whole bunch of dads out there ready to listen. And if you've got a "dad win" you're proud of, share it with us. Your story helps another dad believe he can do it, too.

Thank you for trusting me with your time, your worries, and your hopes. Thank you for letting me be part of your journey. I believe in every dad who picked up this book. You are already making a difference. You are exactly the hero your baby is counting on. You've got this, one day, one diaper, one dad win at a time.

As This Book Helps You With Your Baby...

Whether you learn tips on crying, swaddling, sleep, bonding with your baby, or supporting your partner, we want to hear it. Please leave a review on Amazon.

How To Review This Book:

1. Open your camera app.
2. Scan the QR code above.
3. Wow! The review page opens! (Click the link)
4. Enter a star rating.
5. Share a few words about what you think.

Photos or videos of your experience can help others see how fun and useful this book really is!

REFERENCES

- *Comprehensive Newborn Care Guide for Dads | Delaware WIC* https://delaware.wicresources.org/eat-grow-live-healthy/dads-guide-to-newborn-care/
- *Sleep-Related Infant Deaths: Updated 2022 ...* https://publications.aap.org/pediatrics/article/150/1/e2022057990/188304/Sleep-Related-Infant-Deaths-Updated-2022
- *A Partner's Support During Postpartum Can Literally Be ...* https://www.whattoexpect.com/pregnancy/for-dad/life-after-childbirth.aspx
- *How to Change a Diaper - Expert Tips on Changing a Baby* https://www.daduniversity.com/blog/how-to-change-a-diaper-expert-tips-on-changing-a-baby
- *How Dads Can Support Their Breastfeeding Partner* https://wicbreastfeeding.fns.usda.gov/how-dads-can-support-their-breastfeeding-partner
- *Sleep-Related Infant Deaths: Updated 2022 ...* https://publications.aap.org/pediatrics/article/150/1/e2022057990/188304/Sleep-Related-Infant-Deaths-Updated-2022

- *Baby bath basics: A parent's guide*
  https://www.mayoclinic.org/healthy-lifestyle/infant-
  and-toddler-health/in-depth/healthy-baby/art-20044438
- *8 Hacks for Dealing With Diaper Blowout*
  https://tabeeze.com/blogs/press/diaper-blowout-
  hacks?srsltid=AfmBOor513J1wH8ZChyx6TMu7ZqgW
  ve59yXe8kmYnnLYkM4IcSgPXgHs
- *Prolactin, Oxytocin, and the development of paternal ...*
  https://pmc.ncbi.nlm.nih.gov/articles/PMC3247300/
- *Why Dads and Their Babies Need to Go Skin-to-Skin*
  https://www.scientificamerican.com/article/why-dads-
  and-their-babies-need-to-go-skin-to-skin1/
- *Fun Bonding Activities for Dads and Babies*
  https://childdevelopmentinfo.com/how-to-be-a-
  parent/fun-bonding-activities-for-dads-and-babies/
- *What to do when your baby or toddler only wants Mom
  ...* https://takingcarababies.com/what-to-do-when-your-
  baby-or-toddler-only-wants-mom-or-
  dad?srsltid=AfmBOoqBUW3tnPq6uxEfwlVjvElBJN4
  G284aSPsheCC5SOoqT9_tLR-s
- *How to be a Supportive Postpartum Partner*
  https://boramcare.com/how-to-be-a-supportive-partner-
  during-postpartum/

- *Postpartum depression - Symptoms and causes*
  https://www.mayoclinic.org/diseases-
  conditions/postpartum-depression/symptoms-
  causes/syc-20376617

- *Tips for Postpartum Dads and Partners*
  https://www.postpartum.net/wp-
  content/uploads/2014/11/Tips-for-Postpartum-Dads-
  and-Partners.pdf

- *The Transition to Parenthood: Relationship Tips for
  New ...* https://www.gottman.com/blog/the-transition-
  to-parenthood-relationship-tips-for-new-parents/

- *1 in 10 dads experience postpartum depression, anxiety*
  https://utswmed.org/medblog/paternal-postpartum-
  depression/

- *5 Essential Self-Care Tips for First-Time Dads*
  https://healingspringswellness.com/5-essential-self-
  care-tips-for-first-time-dads-nurturing-your-mental-
  health/

- *Help for Dads | Postpartum Support International (PSI)*
  https://postpartum.net/get-help/help-for-dads/

- *Fatherhood group sessions: A descriptive and
  summative ...*
  https://pmc.ncbi.nlm.nih.gov/articles/PMC7756429/

- *CDC's Developmental Milestones* https://www.cdc.gov/ncbddd/actearly/milestones/index.html

- *Sick baby? When to seek medical attention* https://www.mayoclinic.org/healthy-lifestyle/infant-and-toddler-health/in-depth/healthy-baby/art-20047793

- *Signs of Sleep Regression in Babies and What to Do About It* https://www.whattoexpect.com/first-year/sleep/sleep-regression/

- *Tummy Time* https://www.nationwidechildrens.org/family-resources-education/health-wellness-and-safety-resources/helping-hands/tummy-time

- *Improving your work/life balance as a new dad* https://www.gidgetfoundation.org.au/fact-sheets/improving-your-work-life-balance-as-a-new-dad

- *Morning Routine Tips: Get Out the Door on Time with Kids* https://www.littleones.co/blogs/our-blog/the-morning-how-to-be-organised-and-out-the-door-on-time?srsltid=AfmBOorYYvZNxrhSD65hxowajx9HQmnkPzwyjTEyguxOlGXyCYA5wVwm

- *Tips for Planning Your Return to Work After Parental Leave* https://www.thebump.com/a/returning-to-work-parental-leave

- *Stress Management for Dads: How Your Mental Health ...* https://www.inovanewsroom.org/expert-commentary/2019/06/stress-management-for-dads-how-your-mental-health-impacts-your-kids/
- *The Ultimate First Year Baby Budget* https://wealthkeel.com/blog/first-year-baby-budget/
- *How do I get health insurance for my new baby?* https://www.uhc.com/news-articles/benefits-and-coverage/how-do-i-get-health-insurance-for-my-new-baby
- *Baby Checklist* https://www.cpsc.gov/s3fs-public/206%20Baby%20Safety%20Checklist_web_en NEW.pdf
- *5 Family Traditions for New Babies* https://people.howstuffworks.com/culture-traditions/family-traditions/5-family-traditions-for-new-babies.htm

ABOUT THE AUTHOR

Brad Wells is an enthusiastic advocate for involved fatherhood. With a passion for family dynamics, Brad has researched and written about the transformative journey of fatherhood. He understands the challenges and joys of expecting and caring for a new life, and his experiences have inspired him to share his insights and knowledge with new fathers.

In his latest book, *"DAD, I'M COUNTING ON YOU!: How to Be a Hero in Your Baby's First 12 Months,"* Brad blends practical wisdom with heartfelt stories to guide men through the exhilarating and sometimes overwhelming journey of first-time fatherhood. His comprehensive handbook offers invaluable support and encouragement for fathers navigating the intricacies of their baby's first year.

Brad's writing is characterized by warmth, humor, and relatability, making complex topics accessible to readers of all backgrounds. Through his work, he hopes to empower fathers to embrace their role with confidence, compassion, and a sense of adventure.

When he's not writing, Brad enjoys spending time with his family, watching Netflix, and indulging his love of magic.